Lecture Notes in Computer Science 16369

The series Lecture Notes in Computer Science (LNCS), including its subseries Lecture Notes in Artificial Intelligence (LNAI) and Lecture Notes in Bioinformatics (LNBI), has established itself as a medium for the publication of new developments in computer science and information technology research, teaching, and education.

LNCS enjoys close cooperation with the computer science R & D community, the series counts many renowned academics among its volume editors and paper authors, and collaborates with prestigious societies. Its mission is to serve this international community by providing an invaluable service, mainly focused on the publication of conference and workshop proceedings and postproceedings. LNCS commenced publication in 1973.

Zhigang Li · Yanyan Lan · Zhumin Chen
Editors

Information Retrieval

31st China Conference, CCIR 2025
Shihezi, China, August 15–17, 2025
Revised Selected Papers

Springer

Editors
Zhigang Li
Shihezi University
Xinjiang, China

Yanyan Lan
Tsinghua University
Beijing, China

Zhumin Chen
Shandong University
Jinan, China

ISSN 0302-9743 ISSN 1611-3349 (electronic)
Lecture Notes in Computer Science
ISBN 978-981-95-5636-6 ISBN 978-981-95-5637-3 (eBook)
https://doi.org/10.1007/978-981-95-5637-3

This Springer imprint is published by the registered company Springer Nature Singapore Pte Ltd.
The registered company address is: 152 Beach Road, #21-01/04 Gateway East, Singapore 189721, Singapore

Preface

The 2025 China Conference on Information Retrieval (31st China Conference on Information Retrieval, CCIR 2025), organized by the Chinese Information Processing Society of China (CIPS), was successfully held in Shihezi, Xinjiang on August 15–17, 2025. As the 31 instalments of this conference show, CCIR has established itself as a flagship event in China's information retrieval community, witnessing the growth and innovation of information retrieval technologies.

Research in information retrieval aims to meet the need for fast and accurate access to information and knowledge in the era of data explosion and the rise of artificial intelligence. These research outcomes not only support national strategies but also drive the development of internet and artificial intelligence technologies, significantly enhancing the productivity of society and impacting various aspects of social life.

This conference brought together renowned experts and scholars from around the world and included keynote speeches, themed workshops, poster sessions, and evaluation activities. Additionally, a young scholar forum and cutting-edge workshops on hot research topics were organized.

To ensure the high quality of the conference, the Program Committee organized experts and scholars in the field of information retrieval to rigorously review the submitted papers. The conference received a total of 64 submissions, comprising 51 in Chinese and 13 in English. After the review process, 43 outstanding papers were accepted, with an overall acceptance rate of 67.19%. The acceptance rate for Chinese-language papers was 64.71% (33 papers accepted), and for English-language papers, it was 69.23% (9 papers accepted). All accepted Chinese-language papers will be recommended for publication in relevant academic journals, while the English-language papers are published here in the Springer LNCS series.

CCIR 2025 focused on the deep integration of large language models with classic retrieval paradigms. The conference agenda featured multiple themed workshops and industrial presentations, such as "Advances in LLM Preference Alignment and Knowledge Editing," "Offline Reinforcement Learning and Its Application in Information Recommendation," and "The Application of Large Models in Xiaohongshu's Business." These sessions offered participants extensive opportunities for academic exchange and collaboration, addressing the challenges and opportunities of the new era.

This conference received generous support from numerous organizations and enterprises. We would like to extend our special thanks to our sponsors, Xiaohongshu, Huawei Technologies, Baidu, Inc. and Beijing Bayou Technology Co., Ltd. for their contributions to this conference. Sincere thanks are also due to all the contributors, members of the organizing committee, conference delegates, and volunteers who contributed to the success of CCIR 2025.

The China Conference on Information Retrieval (CCIR) is the most important meeting in China in the field of information retrieval. As the flagship conference of CIPS,

CCIR provides a broad platform for the exchange of the latest academic and technological achievements. The theme of this year's conference, "The Deep Integration of Large Language Models and Classic Retrieval Paradigms," shaped the academic activities. We believe this edition of the event was a complete success, inspiring innovation and fostering collaboration to advance information retrieval technology for national strategies, artificial intelligence progress, and social development.

September 2025

Zhigang Li
Yanyan Lan
Zhumin Chen

Organization

Conference Chairs

Zhigang Li	Shihezi University, China
Zhumin Chen	Shandong University, China
Yanyan Lan	Tsinghua University, China

Program Committee Chairs

Peng Zhang	Tianjin University, China
Zhao Cao	Renmin University of China, China

Organizing Committee Chairs

Changzheng Liu	Shihezi University, China
Yahui Liu	Shihezi University, China

Publicity Chair

Ting Bai	Beijing University of Posts and Telecommunications, China

Publication Chair

Xu Chen	Renmin University of China, China

Web Chair

Qingyao Ai	Tsinghua University, China

Young Forum Chairs

Fan Zhang	Wuhan University, China
Pengjie Ren	Shandong University, China

Evaluation Chairs

Xiaofei Zhu	Chongqing University of Technology, China
Weidong Liu	China Mobile, China

Sponsorship Chairs

Weizhi Ma	Tsinghua University, China
Shen Gao	University of Electronic Science and Technology of China, China

Finance Chair

Peijie Sun	Nanjing University of Posts and Telecommunications, China

Program Committee

Jiawei Chen	Zhejiang University, China
Chuanjun Zhao	Shanxi University of Finance and Economics, China
Hongfei Lin	Dalian University of Technology, China
Chenliang Li	Wuhan University, China
Zhang Yu	Harbin Institute of Technology, China
Hongye Tan	Shanxi University, China
Le Wu	Hefei University of Technology, China
Dan Wu	Wuhan University, China
Bo Xu	Dalian University of Technology, China
Jun Xu	Renmin University of China, China
Xuemeng Song	Southern University of Science and Technology, China

Yanyan Lan	Tsinghua University, China
Peiyu Liu	Shandong Normal University, China
Jianxing Zheng	Shanxi University, China

Contents

CFC-CPI: Cross-Scale Feature Fusion for Compound-Protein Interaction Prediction

Yanfei Li, Qianxi Lin, Zipeng Fan, and Peng Zhang(✉)

College of Intelligence and Computing, Tianjin University, 135 Yaguan Road, Tianjin 300072, China
pzhang@tju.edu.cn

Abstract. To overcome limitations in existing compound representation methods, we propose CFC-CPI, a Cross-scale Feature Fusion approach for compound-protein interaction prediction. CFC-CPI integrates pharmacophore modeling with graph neural networks to represent compounds through atomic-scale (capturing atom types/bonds) and pharmacophore-scale (using BRICS-derived features) graph structures. This dual representation enables comprehensive characterization of compounds' structural and functional properties. Experiments show CFC-CPI achieves state-of-the-art performance across multiple benchmark datasets, outperforming existing models on various metrics. Visualization analyses confirm the model's ability to identify actual compound-protein binding sites, addressing interpretability concerns. In a SARS-CoV-2 virtual screening case study, CFC-CPI demonstrated exceptional performance, suggesting strong potential for drug repurposing applications.

Keywords: Graph Neural Networks · Compound-Protein Interaction · Feature Fusion · Pharmacophore

1 Introduction

The study of Compound Protein Interaction (CPI) is crucial for drug discovery and biomedical research. But CPI measurement is often time-intensive and expensive [25]. Though high-throughput screening (HTS) [18] and virtual screening (VS) [28] are useful, they are limited by cost and time. With AI's success in other fields, researchers are now exploring its use in CPI studies to overcome these challenges. The pharmaceutical industry sees AI tools as a vital "engine" for drug innovation [20]. Using machine learning and neural networks, researchers can analyze large datasets to predict CPI accurately. These AI methods could transform the field by offering efficient, cost-effective CPI prediction, aiding in drug candidate identification and accelerating the drug discovery process [6].

In CPI research, compound representation methods have been a key focus. Many methods leverage the powerful learning capabilities of neural networks to capture important information within compounds, offering new possibilities for

Z. Li et al. (Eds.): CCIR 2025, LNCS 16369, pp. 1–12, 2026.
https://doi.org/10.1007/978-981-95-5637-3_1

CPI prediction and drug design. These methods employ Graph Neural Networks (GNNs) to iteratively update node representations, capturing interactions and information between atoms in compounds. This approach is particularly effective in handling large molecules and complex compounds.

However, most GNN-based approaches to compound modeling often ignore higher-order details like pharmacophores and functional groups [6]. Typically, these methods concentrate on one level of information, missing out on the integration of functional groups and pharmacophores that could reveal molecular properties not yet fully exploited in current atom-based molecular graphs. Pharmacophore modeling is essential in drug design and discovery [27], focusing on identifying structural patterns or functional groups linked to specific drug effects. Pharmacophores, as key structural elements in drug molecules that interact with protein targets, are crucial for drug selectivity and activity. By using pharmacophore modeling, analyzing known active compounds and their associated protein structures can pinpoint key pharmacophoric features. As shown in Fig. 1, a compound aligning with multiple features is deemed to fit the pharmacophore model, which is central to identifying compound-protein interactions [10] [12].

In this paper, inspired by pharmacophore modeling, we propose a cross-scale compound fusion representation approach to comprehensively describe the structure and properties of molecules:

- Our method proposes a novel approach to molecular modeling. The compound is divided into two scales based on atoms and pharmacophores. Each scale's graph captures unique chemical details. This representation leverages structural features and functional characteristics, improving molecule modeling.
- Our experimental results showcase the significant capability of our cross-scale representation approach in the compound-protein interaction task and have revealed the fragments of molecules that interact with proteins through attention mechanisms.
- The experimental results demonstrate that after effective training, CFC-CPI has the potential to discover new drugs.

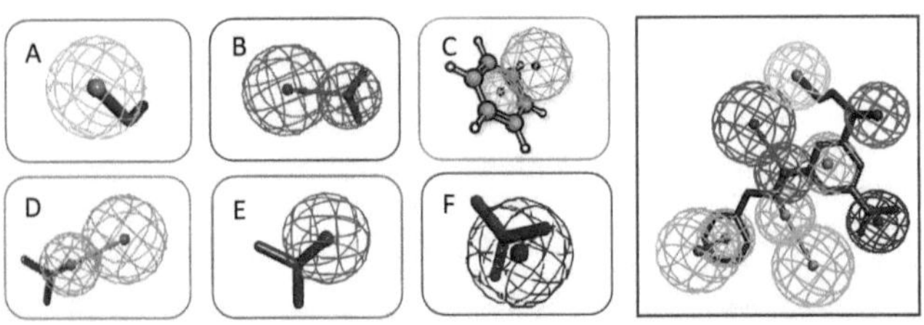

Fig. 1. A signifies the hydrophobic core, B the hydrogen bond donor, C the aromatic ring center, D an additional hydrogen bond donor, and E and F the charged centers. By identifying these pharmacophore features enhances understanding of compound-protein binding.

2 Related Work

In the pursuit of expediting CPI forecasting and enhancing information extraction, deep learning methodologies have become predominant. These can be categorized into three main types: sequence-based, graph-based, and fusion methods.

Sequence-based methods focus on extracting information from protein and molecular sequences. For instance, DeepconvDTI [16] uses CNNs to process protein sequences and molecular fingerprints, while DeepDTA [24] applies CNNs to protein sequences and compound SMILES representations.

Graph-based methods, like GraphDTA [23], directly operate on compound molecular graphs, representing atoms as nodes and bonds as edges, and utilize the graph's structural information for CPI prediction. Both sequence-based and graph-based approaches have achieved commendable performance.

With the advancement of deep learning, various hybrid methodologies have emerged for CPI prediction. TransformerCPI [2] integrates the Transformer architecture to process protein sequences and compound structures, employing self-attention mechanisms to capture long-range dependencies. PerceiverCPI [21] uses cross-attention mechanisms to enhance CPI representation learning and leverages molecular fingerprint information. MulinforCPI [22] utilizes the three-dimensional information of proteins and compounds.

Compared to previous studies, our work presents a novel architecture. By using two scales segmentation, integration, and attention mechanisms, it extracts a broader set of molecular structural and property features and identifies molecular interaction regions.

3 Methodology

This section elaborates on the architecture of the CFC-CPI model as illustrated in Fig. 2. The CFC-CPI model consists of three main components: Protein embedding module, Cross-scale Compound embedding module, and the Final prediction module. The input of Protein embedding model is amino acid sequence of a protein. The Compound embedding module takes the SMILES representation of the compound as input.

3.1 Cross-scale Compound Embedding Learning

Cross-scale Compound Embedding In this subsection, we detail the small molecule representation process. To convert compounds from SMILES format to atom-scale graph representations, we used RDKit [14], a widely-used cheminformatics toolkit. The atom-scale graph is denoted as $G^a = (\mathbf{X}^a, \mathbf{E}^a)$, where $\mathbf{X}^a \in \mathbb{R}^{n_a \times f_{atom}}$ represents atoms. Here, n_a is the number of atoms and f_{atom} is the atom feature dimension. Each atom's features $\mathbf{x}^a \in \mathbf{X}^a$ are encoded via one-hot vectors based on atomic symbol, degree, charge, hybridization, and aromaticity. $\mathbf{E}^a$ represents bonds, with each bond $\mathbf{e}^a \in \mathbf{E}^a$ encoded by a one-hot vector based on bond type.

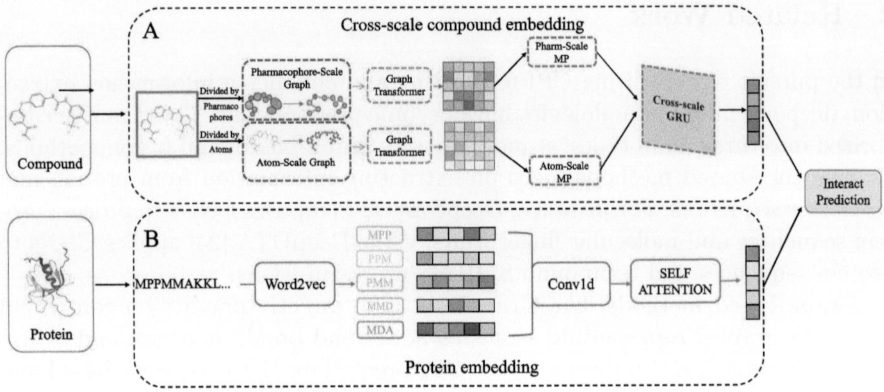

Fig. 2. The framework of CFC-CPI

The pharmacophore-scale graph is generated by fragmenting the atom-scale graph using RDKit's BRICS method, with features summarized in Table 1. This graph is represented as $G^p = (\mathbf{X}^p, \mathbf{E}^p)$, where $\mathbf{X}^p \in \mathbb{R}^{n_p \times f_{pharm}}$ is a collection of n_p pharmacophores, and f_{pharm} is the pharmacophore feature dimension. Each node $\mathbf{x}^p \in \mathbf{X}^p$ is encoded using one-hot vectors based on pharmacophore features, BRICS features, and MACCS fingerprints [7] (Fig. 3). Pharmacophore features include acidity, basicity, and aromaticity. MACCS fingerprints are binary and based on molecular structure and functional groups, aiding in similarity calculations. BRICS features include bonds generated by RDKit. $\mathbf{E}^p$ represents BRICS bonds, with each $\mathbf{e}^p \in \mathbf{E}^p$ encoded via a one-hot vector based on BRICS reaction type.

Message Passing. The atom-scale and pharmacophore-scale graphs are input into separate Graph Transformer layers for feature learning. The Graph Transformer uses multi-headed attention [8] to boost model representation by aggregating diverse features. In this mechanism, the input is split into multiple heads for parallel processing, and their outputs are concatenated to form the final representation for message passing and updating.

Take the atom-scale graph update as an example. The Graph Transformer's input is the node feature matrix $\mathbf{X}^a = [\mathbf{x}_1, \mathbf{x}_2, \ldots, \mathbf{x}_{n_a}] \in \mathbb{R}^{n_a \times f_{atom}}$ of graph G^a, where n_a is the number of nodes and f_{atom} the feature dimension. We compute $\mathbf{Q}_h^l = \mathbf{x}_i^l \mathbf{W}_h^Q$, $\mathbf{K}_h^l = \mathbf{x}_i^l \mathbf{W}_h^K$, $\mathbf{V}_h^l = \mathbf{x}_i^l \mathbf{W}_h^V$, where h is the head index, l the layer index, and $\mathbf{W}_Q, \mathbf{W}_K, \mathbf{W}_V \in \mathbb{R}^{f_a \times d_k}$ are weight matrices. Node features are updated via multi-headed attention.

$$\varphi^l i = \sum_{j \in N(i)} \text{Multihead}(\mathbf{Q}^{l-1}, \mathbf{K}^{l-1}, \mathbf{V}^{l-1}) * \mathbf{W}^l(\mathbf{x}_j^{l-1}) \quad (1)$$

$$\mathbf{x}_i^l = \sigma\left(\mathbf{W}^l * \text{Concat}(\mathbf{x}^{l-1} i, \varphi^l i)\right), \quad \mathbf{x}_i^0 = \mathbf{x}_i \quad (2)$$

Table 1. Pharmacophore-scale graph features

Pharmacophore features	hydrogen bond acceptors, hydrogen bond donors aromatic groups, hydrophobic regions
BRICS feature	element types, connection modes the number of rings in the substructures
MACCS fingerprint	rings, functional groups

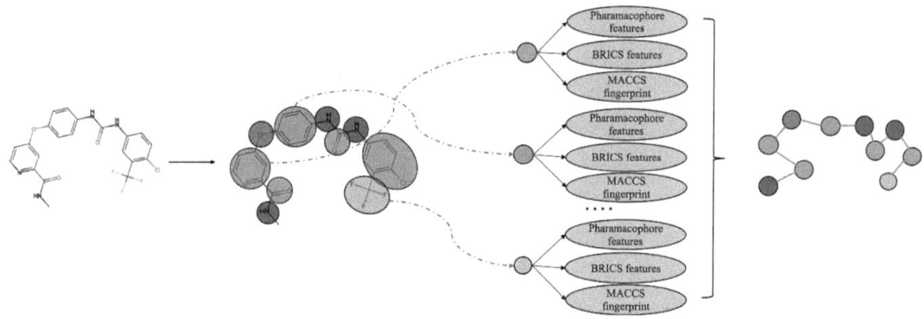

Fig. 3. Framework of Pharmacophore-scale Graph: The molecular graph is divided into Pharmacophore-scale Graphs consisting of multiple pharmacophores using the BRICS rule in RDKit. Each pharmacophore serves as a node in the graph, and each node contains pharmacophore features, BRICS features, and MACCS fingerprints. The nodes are connected by BRICS bonds generated using RDKit.

where $\mathbf{W}^l$ is a learnable weight matrix, $N(i)$ denotes node i's neighbors, and $Concat()$ concatenates head vectors. Multihead is calculated as:

$$\mathbf{head}_i^l = \text{Softmax}\left(\frac{\mathbf{Q}_h^l \mathbf{K}_h^l}{\sqrt{d_k}}\right) \mathbf{V}_h^l \tag{3}$$

$$\text{MultiHead}(\mathbf{Q}^l, \mathbf{K}^l, \mathbf{V}^l) = \text{Concat}(\mathbf{head}_1^l, \ldots, \mathbf{head}_H^l)\mathbf{W}_O \tag{4}$$

Here, H is the number of attention heads, and d_k is the dimension of $\mathbf{K}$. The pharmacophore-scale graph is updated similarly.

Final Molecule Embedding Fusion. To obtain a molecule's feature vector, we aggregate updated graph data using a Gate Recurrent Unit (GRU), a variant of Recurrent Neural Networks (RNNs) [26]. The updated node feature matrices for the atom-scale graph G^a and pharmacophore-scale graph G^p are $\mathbf{X}^a \in \mathbb{R}^{n_a \times f_a}$ and $\mathbf{X}^p \in \mathbb{R}^{n_p \times f_p}$, respectively. We fuse these scales via multi-head attention to form the input matrix $\mathbf{X}$:

$$\mathbf{X} = \mathbf{V}^a + \text{MultiHead}(\mathbf{Q}^a, \mathbf{K}^p, \mathbf{V}^p)$$

where $\mathbf{Q}^a = \mathbf{X}^a W_Q$, $\mathbf{K}^p = \mathbf{X}^p W_K$, $\mathbf{V}^p = \mathbf{X}^p W_V$, with $\mathbf{W}_Q \in \mathbb{R}^{f_a \times d_k}$, $\mathbf{W}_K, \mathbf{W}_V \in \mathbb{R}^{f_p \times d_k}$ as weight matrices.

The GRU processes this fused information to generate the molecular feature vector. The key equations are:

$$r_i = \sigma(\mathbf{W}_r \cdot [\mathbf{h}_{i-1}, \mathbf{x}_i])$$
$$z_i = \sigma(\mathbf{W}_z \cdot [\mathbf{h}_{i-1}, \mathbf{x}_i])$$
$$\hat{\mathbf{h}}_i = \tanh(\mathbf{W}_h \cdot [r_i \odot \mathbf{h}_{i-1}, \mathbf{x}_i])$$
$$\mathbf{h}_i = (1 - z_i) \odot \mathbf{h}_{i-1} + z_i \odot \hat{\mathbf{h}}_i$$

Here, σ is the sigmoid function, $\mathbf{h}_i$ is the hidden state of node i, z_i is the update gate, r_i is the reset gate, and $\hat{\mathbf{h}}_i$ is the candidate hidden state. The final hidden state $\mathbf{h}_{n_a}$ serves as the molecule's feature vector.

This GRU-based approach effectively combines neighbor node features, capturing molecular characteristics comprehensively. By integrating update gates, reset gates, and attention mechanisms, the model enhances molecular structure and property modeling, leading to a more accurate representation of molecular features.

3.2 Protein Sequence Representation Learning

To process a protein sequence $S = \{s_1, s_2, ..., s_{L_p}\}$, where L_p is the sequence length and s_i is the i-th amino acid, we use the k-mer method to segment it into subsequences $R = \{r_1, r_2, ..., r_{Nr}\}$, with $Nr = L_p - n + 1$. For example, $n = 3$ splits *MPPMMDAKKKL* into *MPP*, *PPM*, etc., capturing local context.

We then use word2vec [19] to convert these subsequences into real-valued embedding vectors $\mathbf{R} = \{\mathbf{r}_1, \mathbf{r}_2, ..., \mathbf{r}_{Nr}\}$, where $\mathbf{r}_i \in \mathbb{R}^{Hp}$ and Hp is the embedding dimension.

Next, we apply one-dimensional convolutional layers with GLU activation and residual connections to extract local features, updating $\mathbf{R}$ to have dimension Cp.

Finally, a self-attention mechanism is used to model correlations between subsequences, followed by layer normalization to produce the final protein representation $\mathbf{p} \in \mathbb{R}^{Np \times 1}$:

$$\mathbf{p} = \text{LayerNorm}(\text{SelfAttention}(\mathbf{R}))$$

3.3 Final Prediction Module

In the CPI prediction task, the final output is to predict whether a compound and a protein interact or not.

After obtaining the final vector $\mathbf{h}_{n_a}$ for the compound and final vector $\mathbf{p}$ for the protein, the two are concatenated and fed into a fully connected network with ReLU activation [30] to enhance model representation power and nonlinear fitting capability to compose the prediction module and output the final result *out*:

$$out = \text{MLP}(\text{ReLU}(\text{MLP}(\text{concat}(\mathbf{h}_{n_a}, \mathbf{p})))) \tag{5}$$

$$\text{MLP} : \mathbf{y} = \sigma(\mathbf{W}\mathbf{x} + \mathbf{b}) \tag{6}$$

where $\mathbf{y}$ is the output vector, $\mathbf{W}$ is the weight matrix, $\mathbf{b}$ is the bias vector, and $\sigma(\cdot)$ is the activation function.

4 Experiments

4.1 Compare with Orther Modules

We selected classical methods and SOTA methods as baselines. DeepDTA [24], DeepConvDTI [16], GraphDTA [23],and TransformerCPI [2] are four well-known methods. Additionally, we included four recent methods: Hyper AttentionDTI [32], CPGL [31], PerceiverCPI [21], and MulinforCPI [22].

4.2 Performance on Label Reversal Binary Classification Datasets

The GPCR and Kinase datasets were curated specifically with a focus on label reversal experiments. In essence, these experiments involve a compound being assigned to one class in the training set, while intentionally designating it to the opposing class in the test set. This methodology aims to challenge and enhance models' ability to accurately learn and predict how compounds interact with proteins.

In the GPCR dataset, CFC-CPI demonstrated superior performance, achieving the highest AUC (Area Under the Curve) and PRC (Precision-Recall Curve) values compared to all baseline methods. Specifically, CFC-CPI surpassed previous best results by an improvement of 0.9% in AUC and 2.2% in PRC.

Similarly, for the Kinase dataset, CFC-CPI achieved the second-highest AUC while attaining the optimal PRC. Notably, CFC-CPI's PRC surpassed the previous best results by 0.4%, while its AUC decreased slightly by 0.8% in comparison.

These findings highlight the effectiveness of CFC-CPI in handling complex protein-compound interactions, especially in scenarios where label reversal experiments are employed to rigorously evaluate model performance (Table 2).

4.3 Performance on Novel Pair Experiment

Following MulinforCPI, we conducted novel pair regression experiments on the Davis dataset using 5-fold cross-cluster validation. In this setting, neither the training compound nor the training protein appeared in the test set. We employ Mean Squared Error (MSE), Confidence Interval (CI), and Spearman Correlation as metrics to evaluate the models. The results in Table 3 demonstrate that CFC-CPI achieved the best MSE and CI among all models and performed comparably to the SOTA method MulinforCPI. A high CI denotes a model's strong predictive power, a favorable attribute in predictive modeling.

Table 2. Performance of HyperCPI and baselines on GPCR and Kinase

Method	GPCR		Kinase	
	AUC	PRC	AUC	PRC
CPI-GNN	0.490	0.528	0.445	0.173
GCN	0.820	0.809	0.447	0.186
GraphDTA	0.825	0.817	0.434	0.171
TransformerCPI	0.863	0.859	0.598	0.280
HyperAttentionDTI	0.851	0.841	0.296	0.162
CPGL	0.856	0.861	**0.691**	0.342
PerceiverCPI	0.870	0.826	0.464	0.276
MulinforCPI	0.840	0.834	0.622	0.267
CFC-CPI	**0.879**	**0.881**	0.683	**0.346**

Table 3. Performance for novel pair experiments on Davis dataset.

Method	MSE	CI	Spearman Correlation
DeepDTA	0.719($\pm$ 0.312)	0.456($\pm$ 0.107)	-0.054($\pm$ 0.162)
DeepConvDTI	0.602($\pm$ 0.221)	0.580($\pm$ 0.065)	0.141($\pm$ 0.105)
GraphDTA	1.078($\pm$ 0.564)	0.499($\pm$ 0.100)	0.011($\pm$ 0.139)
TransformerCPI	0.565($\pm$ 0.252)	0.552($\pm$ 0.024)	0.087($\pm$ 0.037)
HyperattentionDTI	0.633($\pm$ 0.249)	0.529($\pm$ 0.046)	0.049($\pm$ 0.078)
PerceiverCPI	0.668($\pm$ 0.357)	0.547($\pm$ 0.071)	0.062($\pm$ 0.124)
MulinforCPI	0.547($\pm$ 0.256)	0.646($\pm$ 0.050)	**0.237($\pm$ 0.061)**
CFC-CPI	**0.524($\pm$ 0.341)**	**0.712($\pm$ 0.121)**	0.214($\pm$ 0.103)

4.4 Ablation Experiment

To evaluate our CFC-CPI approach, we first established a baseline using a three-layer GCN for compound feature extraction, keeping the protein embedding and prediction module consistent with CFC-CPI. As shown in Table 4, the baseline achieved AUC-ROC scores of 0.927 (Human [15]), 0.924 (C.elegans [1]), and 0.796 (GPCR).

We then assessed Model-A (Atom-scale) and Model-B (pharmacophore-scale) individually. Both significantly outperformed the baseline, confirming their importance in CPI prediction. The Atom-scale module, leveraging a Graph-Transformer network, focuses on overall molecular structure and chemical properties, improving performance by 3% (Human), 4.1% (C.elegans), and 2.7% (GPCR). The pharmacophore-scale module emphasizes pharmacophore features like hydrogen bond acceptors and aromatic groups, which are critical for high-precision CPI.

Table 4. The Ablation Study Results, which include AUC-ROC values, were obtained on three public datasets: C. elegans, Human, and GPCR. AS:Atom-scale.PS:Pharmascophore-scale.

Method	AS	PS	Human	C.elegans	GPCR
Baseline	×	×	0.927	0.924	0.796
Model-A	√	×	0.957↑	0.963↑	0.823↑
Model-B	×	√	0.943↑	0.941↑	0.821↑
CFC-CPI	√	√	**0.988↑**	**0.996↑**	**0.883↑**

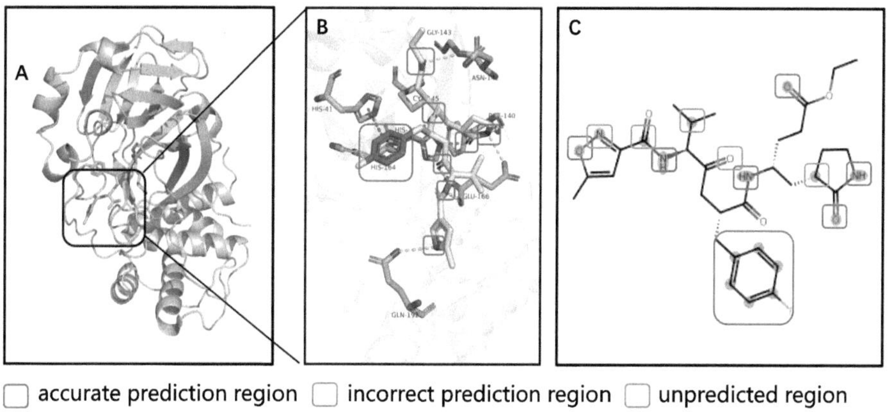

Fig. 4. Visualization of the interaction between SARS-CoV-2 3CL protease and rupintrivir compound includes the following components: (A) an overview image showing the overall interaction, (B) a magnified image depicting the interaction between the compound and the amino acids in the binding region of the protein, with the red box indicating the specific portion where the compound interacts, and (C) the red-colored portion is the atoms of the compound that obtained high attention scores in the graph transformer model. (Color figure online)

Finally, combining both scales in CFC-CPI further enhanced performance, surpassing all previous configurations. This validates our approach's effectiveness.

4.5 Visualisation

We used the GraphTransformer's attention weights to visualize compound-protein interactions. Using the SARS-CoV-2 3CL-Pro and rupintrivir compound as inputs, we generated an attention weight graph (Fig. 4C), where red highlights indicate higher attention weights, aiding CPI analysis.

We also employed the Pymol toolkit to visualize the compound-protein interaction (Fig. 4A). Figure 4B zooms in on the interaction, with dashed lines representing bonds between the compound and protein. Purple lines denote pi-pi bonds (aromatic ring interactions), and yellow lines indicate hydrogen bonds. In Fig. 4B, 13 binding sites correspond to multiple positions in Fig. 4C. Of these, 12 were successfully predicted (red boxes), 3 were incorrectly predicted (blue boxes), and 2 were missed (green circles).

These results show that CFC-CPI, with pharmacophore information, enhances CPI analysis, which is highly valuable for drug design and discovery. Visualizing outcomes helps identify key interaction components, and incorporating pharmacophore details into CPI prediction models holds great promise for future research.

4.6 Case Study

To demonstrate CFC-CPI's performance in virtual screening, we chose the SARS-CoV-2 3C-like Protease as the target. We obtained SMILES data for 100 common drugs from DrugOOD [11] and the 3CLPro sequence from PubChem [13] and UniProt [3]. These were input into CFC-CPI, which predicted the top 7 compounds with the highest interaction potential and one with the lowest. The interaction probabilities, reflecting interaction likelihood, are shown in Table 5.

Table 5. Results of CFC-CPI in practical virtual screening experiments.

Molecules	Predicted probability (%)	*Source*
Enfuvirtide	98.6	
Rupintrivir	96.5	[17]
Amprenavir	94.7	[5]
Remdesivir	93.3	[9]
Tipranavir	89.3	[5]
Cefprozil	84.3	
Ritonavir	80.3	[4]
Aspirin	4.7	

Table 5 shows that Amprenavir, Rupintrivir, Remdesivir, Tipranavir, and Ritonavir have high interaction potential with 3CLPro, aligning with existing research and clinical trials. Conversely, drugs like Aspirin showed minimal interaction potential and were deemed unrelated [29]. These results validate CFC-CPI's effectiveness and reliability in new drug prediction, underscoring its utility in research and drug discovery.

References

1. Brenner, S.: The genetics of caenorhabditis elegans. Genetics **77**(1), 71–94 (1974)

2. Chen, L.: Transformercpi: improving compound-protein interaction prediction by sequence-based deep learning with self-attention mechanism and label reversal experiments. Bioinformatics **36**(16), 4406–4414 (2020)
3. Consortium, U.: Uniprot: a worldwide hub of protein knowledge. Nucleic Acids Res. **47**(D1), D506–D515 (2019)
4. Costanzo: Sars-cov-2: recent reports on antiviral therapies based on lopinavir/ritonavir, darunavir/umifenovir, hydroxychloroquine, remdesivir, favipiravir and other drugs for the treatment of the new coronavirus. Current medicinal chemistry **27**(27), 4536–4541 (2020)
5. Dayer, M.R.: Old drugs for newly emerging viral disease, covid-19: Bioinformatic prospective. arXiv preprint arXiv:2003.04524 (2020)
6. Du, B.X., Qin, Y., Jiang, Y.F., Xu, Y., Yiu, S.M., Yu, H., Shi, J.Y.: Compound-protein interaction prediction by deep learning: databases, descriptors and models. Drug Discovery Today **27**(5), 1350–1366 (2022)
7. Durant, J.L., Leland, B.A., Henry, D.R., Nourse, J.G.: Reoptimization of mdl keys for use in drug discovery. J. Chem. Inf. Comput. Sci. **42**(6), 1273–1280 (2002)
8. Dwivedi, V.P., Bresson, X.: A generalization of transformer networks to graphs. arXiv preprint arXiv:2012.09699 (2020)
9. Elfiky, A.A.: Ribavirin, remdesivir, sofosbuvir, galidesivir, and tenofovir against sars-cov-2 rna dependent rna polymerase (rdrp): A molecular docking study. Life Sci. **253**, 117592 (2020)
10. Giordano, D., Biancaniello, C., Argenio, M.A., Facchiano, A.: Drug design by pharmacophore and virtual screening approach. Pharmaceuticals **15**(5), 646 (2022)
11. Ji, Y., et al.: Drugood: Out-of-distribution (ood) dataset curator and benchmark for ai-aided drug discovery–a focus on affinity prediction problems with noise annotations. arXiv preprint arXiv:2201.09637 (2022)
12. Jiang, Y., et al.: Pharmacophoric-constrained heterogeneous graph transformer model for molecular property prediction. Commun. Chem. **6**(1), 60 (2023)
13. Kim, S., Chen, J., Cheng, T., Gindulyte, A., He, J., He, S., Li, Q., Shoemaker, B.A., Thiessen, P.A., Yu, B., et al.: Pubchem 2019 update: improved access to chemical data. Nucleic Acids Res. **47**(D1), D1102–D1109 (2019)
14. Landrum, G., et al.: Rdkit: a software suite for cheminformatics, computational chemistry, and predictive modeling. Greg Landrum **8**, 31 (2013)
15. Lappalainen, T., Sammeth, M., Friedländer, M.R., et al.: Transcriptome and genome sequencing uncovers functional variation in humans. Nature **501**(7468), 506–511 (2013)
16. Lee, I., Keum, J., Nam, H.: Deepconv-dti: prediction of drug-target interactions via deep learning with convolution on protein sequences. PLoS Comput. Biol. **15**(6), e1007129 (2019)
17. Lockbaum, G.J., et al.: Pan-3c protease inhibitor rupintrivir binds sars-cov-2 main protease in a unique binding mode. Biochemistry **60**(39), 2925–2931 (2021)
18. Macarron, R., et al.: Impact of high-throughput screening in biomedical research. Nat. Rev. Drug Discovery **10**(3), 188–195 (2011)
19. Mikolov, T., Chen, K., Corrado, G., Dean, J.: Efficient estimation of word representations in vector space. arXiv preprint arXiv:1301.3781 (2013)
20. Nagra, N.S., Bleys, J., Champagne, D., Devereson, A., Macak, M.: Understanding the company landscape in ai-driven biopharma r&d
21. Nguyen, N.Q., Jang, G., Kim, H., Kang, J.: Perceiver cpi: a nested cross-attention network for compound–protein interaction prediction. Bioinformatics **39**(1), btac731 (2023)

22. Nguyen, N.Q., Park, S., Gim, M., Kang, J.: Mulinforcpi: enhancing precision of compound–protein interaction prediction through novel perspectives on multi-level information integration. Briefings Bioinform. **25**(1), bbad484 (2024)
23. Nguyen, T., Le, H., Quinn, T.P., Nguyen, T., Le, T.D., Venkatesh, S.: Graphdta: predicting drug-target binding affinity with graph neural networks. Bioinformatics **37**(8), 1140–1147 (2021)
24. Öztürk, H., Özgür, A., Ozkirimli, E.: Deepdta: deep drug-target binding affinity prediction. Bioinformatics **34**(17), i821–i829 (2018)
25. Paul, S.M., Mytelka, D.S., Dunwiddie, C.T., Persinger, C.C., Munos, B.H., Lindborg, S.R., Schacht, A.L.: How to improve r&d productivity: the pharmaceutical industry's grand challenge. Nat. Rev. Drug Discovery **9**(3), 203–214 (2010)
26. Schuster, M., Paliwal, K.K.: Bidirectional recurrent neural networks. IEEE Trans. Signal Process. **45**(11), 2673–2681 (1997)
27. Seidel, T., Schuetz, D.A., Garon, A., Langer, T.: The pharmacophore concept and its applications in computer-aided drug design. Progress in the Chemistry of Organic Natural Products 110: Cheminformatics in Natural Product Research pp. 99–141 (2019)
28. Spyrakis, F., Cavasotto, C.N.: Open challenges in structure-based virtual screening: receptor modeling, target flexibility consideration and active site water molecules description. Arch. Biochem. Biophys. **583**, 105–119 (2015)
29. Wijaya, I., Andhika, R., Huang, I., Purwiga, A., Budiman, K.Y.: The effects of aspirin on the outcome of covid-19: a systematic review and meta-analysis. Clinical Epidemiology Global Health **12**, 100883 (2021)
30. Yarotsky, D.: Error bounds for approximations with deep relu networks. Neural Netw. **94**, 103–114 (2017)
31. Zhao, M., Yuan, M., Yang, Y., Xu, S.X.: Cpgl: prediction of compound-protein interaction by integrating graph attention network with long short-term memory neural network. IEEE/ACM Trans. Comput. Biol. Bioinform. (2022)
32. Zhao, Q., Zhao, H., Zheng, K., Wang, J.: Hyperattentiondti: improving drug-protein interaction prediction by sequence-based deep learning with attention mechanism. Bioinformatics **38**(3), 655–662 (2022)

Reinforcement Learning-Based Attribute Alignment for Role-Playing of LLMs

Jiayang Fan and Ting Bai(✉)

Beijing University of Posts and Telecommunications, Beijing 100876, China
{fjy01,baiting}@bupt.edu.cn

Abstract. Role-playing agents are becoming increasingly crucial in interactive AI systems, yet current approaches mainly rely on prompt engineering or fine-tuning to condition agents on predefined character profiles. These methods typically encounter challenges in maintaining fine-grained attribute alignment and handling low-knowledge scenarios, often leading to inconsistent role expressions across diverse contexts and when background information is limited. To overcome these limitations, we propose Attribute-Aligned Policy Optimization (AAPO), a reinforcement learning framework that integrates Direct Preference Optimization (DPO) or Proximal Policy Optimization (PPO) to explicitly strengthen the alignment between agent behaviors and role attributes, enabling faithful maintenance of role personality, language style, and background traits. Experiments demonstrate that AAPO significantly outperforms prompt-based and fine-tuning baselines in both LLM automated evaluations and human evaluations. Notably, AAPO exhibits consistent superiority in high-knowledge and low-knowledge settings, ensuring stable attribute adherence even under limited role information.

Keywords: Role-playing Agents · Reinforcement Learning · Large Language Model

1 Introduction

The rapid advancement of large language models has significantly enhanced the development of interactive AI systems, among which role-playing agents have attracted increasing attention [1–4]. These agents simulate fictional or real-world characters, offering immersive and personalized user experiences across domains such as virtual companionship, education, and entertainment [5–7]. However, ensuring that an agent consistently embodies a predefined character profile—including personality, speaking style, emotional traits, and relational behavior—remains a critical challenge.

Current methods for constructing role-playing agents primarily rely on prompt engineering [8–10] or supervised fine-tuning on profile-conditioned dialogues [11–14]. While these approaches achieve initial success, they commonly suffer from three major limitations: (1) Existing models often fail to maintain

Z. Li et al. (Eds.): CCIR 2025, LNCS 16369, pp. 13–25, 2026.
https://doi.org/10.1007/978-981-95-5637-3_2

attribute consistency across diverse dialogue contexts. It is difficult to ensure that agents accurately and granularly follow specific personality, style traits, and other role attributes across diverse scenarios, leading to significant variability and instability in role attribute expressions across different contexts. (2) Low character consistency under different scenarios: it is difficult to ensure fine-grained adherence to specified personality and style traits across diverse scenarios, like different time nodes and locations; (3) Poor performance under low-knowledge contexts, where agents struggle to maintain persona coherence with limited background information, causing significant fluctuations in attribute alignment.

Recent studies, such as Beyond Dialogue [15] and RoleLLM [8], highlight the importance of fine-grained profile-dialogue alignment to mitigate these issues. Nevertheless, most solutions still treat attributes alignment as a supervised learning problem, without leveraging the dynamic adaptation capabilities inherent to reinforcement learning. To address these challenges, we propose Attribute-Aligned Policy Optimization (AAPO), a reinforcement learning framework that explicitly enhances the alignment between agent behaviors and predefined role profiles. Specifically, we integrate Direct Preference Optimization (DPO) [16] or Proximal Policy Optimization (PPO) [17] to train agents that can dynamically optimize for both dialogue naturalness and profile consistency during interactive generation. Our method introduces task-specific rewards that encourage specific attribute adherence while maintaining conversational fluency.

Through extensive experiments across both high-knowledge and low-knowledge settings, we demonstrate that AAPO-trained LLMs significantly outperform prompt-based and fine-tuned baselines. Moreover, AAPO enables controllable trade-offs between attribute fidelity and response quality, providing a flexible mechanism for adaptive deployment of role-playing agents with LLMs.

In summary, our contributions are as follows:

- To address the issue of poor attribute alignment in existing methods, we propose a reinforcement learning approach that ensures consistency in role-playing across diverse scenarios and under low-knowledge conditions.
- We propose AAPO, a novel reinforcement learning framework with DPO or PPO technique, to explicitly optimize for fine-grained attribute alignment in role-playing dialogues.
- Comprehensive experiments demonstrate that our AAPO significantly improves the attribute alignment compared to existing baselines.

2 Related Work

As role-playing agents become increasingly prevalent in interactive AI systems, ensuring that agents consistently adhere to predefined character profiles throughout dialogues has emerged as a key research challenge. Existing work has primarily focused on three aspects: the construction of role-playing agents, methods for improving profile alignment, and the application of reinforcement learning in language model training. In the following, we review progress in these areas and clarify the positioning of our approach within the broader landscape.

2.1 Role-Playing Agents

The development of role-playing agents has gained significant momentum with the rise of large language models. Early approaches focused on constructing datasets manually or by extracting dialogues from novels and scripts [12,18], conditioning models through simple persona prompts. Recent efforts, such as CharacterGLM [9] and RoleLLM [8], attempt to build more sophisticated agents by fine-tuning models on persona-conditioned dialogues. However, these methods often fail to guarantee fine-grained consistency across multi-turn interactions, leading to drift from the intended character traits over time.

Recent work by Bai et al. [19] introduces BaiJia, the largest role-playing agent platform featuring over 19,000 Chinese historical characters. Unlike prior systems that rely on fictional or modern profiles, BaiJia focuses on low-resource historical characters, addressing challenges in fragmented textual sources and cultural consistency. Through structured resume construction and dialogue generation, it enhances persona grounding and evaluative benchmarks. While BaiJia targets historical and heritage-specific agents, our work complements it by proposing a reinforcement learning-based optimization framework (AAPO) that addresses controllability and attribute alignment in both knowledge-rich and knowledge-sparse scenarios.

2.2 Profile Alignment and Consistency

Maintaining profile alignment is crucial for realistic and immersive role-playing interactions. Existing studies explore various ways to represent role traits, such as predefined MBTI personality types [1], speaking styles, emotional states, and relationship dynamics [11,20]. However, the majority of approaches apply static fine-tuning, which does not generalize well when background knowledge is sparse or novel scenarios are encountered. To address profile-dialogue mismatches, Yu et al. [15] proposed Beyond Dialogue, a framework that introduces sentence-level alignment tasks to ensure closer adherence between dialogue and role profiles. While effective, these methods primarily rely on supervised learning and lack mechanisms for dynamic adaptation during generation.

Recent benchmarks, including CharacterEval [21] and DITTO [22], emphasize the need for consistent persona expression even under unseen conditions, highlighting the gap between current fine-tuning methods and the demands of robust role-playing applications.

2.3 Reinforcement Learning for Language Models

Reinforcement learning has emerged as a powerful technique to refine language models beyond supervised objectives. Reinforcement Learning from Human Feedback (RLHF) [23] demonstrated that policies trained with preference-based feedback significantly improve helpfulness and alignment. Subsequent works, such as Direct Preference Optimization (DPO) [16] and Offline RLHF methods [24], propose more efficient, stable ways to incorporate preference signals

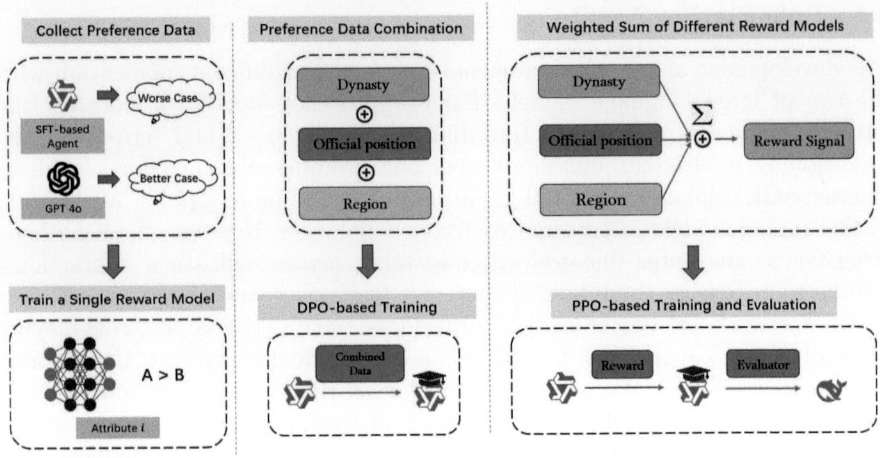

Fig. 1. Framework of our AAPO with DPO or PPO RL Training.

without costly online interactions. Although RL methods have been widely adopted for general-purpose instruction following [2,25], their application in role-playing agents remains underexplored. Integrating RL techniques to specifically optimize for profile adherence represents a promising yet largely untapped research direction.

In this work, we build on these advances by introducing Attribute-Aligned Policy Optimization (AAPO), which for the first time systematically combines DPO and PPO to strengthen attribute-level consistency in role-playing agents. Unlike prior methods that passively rely on supervised persona conditioning, AAPO actively optimizes for dynamic, fine-grained profile adherence across diverse and knowledge-sparse scenarios, pushing the boundaries of controllable and reliable role-playing AI.

3 Our Framework

In this section, we present the design of our Attribute-Aligned Policy Optimization (AAPO) framework for training role-playing agents, which leverages reinforcement learning to achieve fine-grained control over agent behaviors. Our approach allows for two training configurations: Direct Preference Optimization (DPO) or Proximal Policy Optimization (PPO), each serving a distinct purpose depending on the training objectives.

3.1 Framework Overview

The overview architecture of our AAPO framework is shown in Fig. 1. It consists of three main components: supervised fine-tuning, preference data construction for DPO Fine-tuning, and attribute reward model for PPO optimization.

Supervised Fine-Tuning. We begin by initializing the agent with supervised fine-tuning (SFT) using a dataset of persona-conditioned dialogues. This ensures the agent has a basic understanding of language generation and initial exposure to character attributes.

Preference Data Construction. We construct preference data for DPO training by leveraging the SFT model outputs as negative samples and generating positive samples using GPT-4o with carefully designed prompts. Specifically:

- **Negative Samples**: Generated by the SFT model, which lacks preference optimization and may produce responses that partially align with the intended persona but exhibit inconsistencies.
- **Positive Samples**: Generated using GPT-4o, guided by carefully designed prompts that explicitly encourage adherence to predefined persona attributes, ensuring high-quality, consistent responses.

Attribute Reward Model. We design distinct reward models for each attribute, each evaluating aspects such as character consistency, linguistic style, historical context adaptation, and social behavior compliance within the respective attribute's framework. Each reward model is trained using attribute-specific criteria and automatically scores the agent's responses during PPO training.

Reinforcement Learning Optimization. The reinforcement learning-enhanced approach enables the agent to maintain a high degree of attribute fidelity while ensuring natural and engaging dialogue interactions. Depending on the training strategy, we utilize either DPO or PPO:

- **DPO Fine-Tuning**: We mix preference data proportionally based on their quantity in the training set, ensuring that the agent learns balanced attribute representations. For each preference pair (positive vs. negative), the DPO objective is defined as:

$$\mathcal{L}_{\text{DPO}} = -\log \sigma\left(\beta\left(\log \pi(a^+|s) - \log \pi(a^-|s)\right)\right), \tag{1}$$

where π is the agent's policy, σ denotes the sigmoid function, and β is a scaling factor. $\log \pi(a^+|s)$ denotes the logarithmic probabilities of the model generating the preferred actions under state s. $\log \pi(a^-|s)$ denotes the logarithmic probabilities of the model generating the dispreferred actions under state s.

- **PPO Reward Optimization**: We refine the agent using a weighted multi-attribute reward model. Specifically, in our role-playing task, we employ reward models for the following three key attributes: dynasty, official position, and region. The dynasty defines historical context (e.g., Tang norms), official position dictates social tone (e.g., Chinese emperor), and region shapes linguistic style (e.g., Jiangnan traits).

$$R_{\text{total}} = \alpha R_{\text{dynasty}} + \beta R_{\text{official}} + \gamma R_{\text{region}}, \tag{2}$$

where R_{dynasty}, R_{official}, and R_{region} are the reward models designed for the dynasty, official position, and region attributes, respectively. $\alpha = 0.3$, $\beta = 0.4$, $\gamma = 0.3$ are the weights of the reward models. This setup allows the role-playing agent to dynamically optimize for multiple profile traits during dialogue generation.

3.2 Training Procedure

We initialize the agent with supervised fine-tuning using persona-conditioned dialogue data. Preference data is constructed using SFT outputs as negative samples and GPT-4o responses (generated with designed prompts) as positive samples. Depending on the training strategy, we employ two distinct reinforcement learning strategies:

- DPO-based fine-tuning with proportional preference data mixing,
- PPO-based optimization using a weighted multi-attribute reward model.

This flexible reinforcement learning strategy ensures that the role-playing agent achieves fine-grained profile consistency (through DPO) or adaptive attribute optimization (through PPO).

4 Experiment

4.1 Experimental Setup

Datasets. We conduct our experiments on two benchmark datasets:

- **BaiJia Benchmark** [19]: A large-scale benchmark for role-playing with Chinese historical characters, which provides character dialogues for STF and character evaluations.
- **Character-LLM Benchmark** [11]: A benchmark for multi-turn dialogues with diverse role-playing scenarios, designed to assess the agent's ability to maintain persona consistency, values, and other traits.

Baseline Models. We compare our AAPO framework against several representative baseline models, including:

- **ChatGLM-6B, Qwen2.5-7B, and LLaMA3-8B**: Large-scale language models fine-tuned with supervised learning [9,26,27].
- **Baichuan-NPC and Xingchen**: Role-playing models designed for historical or fictional characters [28,29].
- **SFT Variants**: Our model with supervised fine-tuning only, and with various reward model combinations.

Table 1. BaiJia Evaluation Metrics for Dialogue

Metric	Description
CC	Character Consistency: Measures the agent's ability to maintain a consistent persona, including adherence to predefined personality traits and behaviors.
EI	Authentic Emotional Expression and Intellectual Depth and Philosophical Views
DA	Coherence and Logicality of Dialogue and Interactivity in Dialogue
CR	Character Personality and Innovative Thinking and Further Development of Character Complexity
CHA	Language Style Matching Character Identity, Era Strict Alignment with Historical and Cultural Views of the Era
CA	Charm and Attractiveness of the Character and Emotional Impact in Character Interactions

4.2 Evaluation Strategy

In this section, we detail the evaluation methods used in our framework to assess the performance of role-playing agents. Our evaluation design is informed by two recent studies—BaiJia [19] and Character-LLM [11]—which provide comprehensive metrics for measuring the quality of role-playing interactions. The evaluation metrics of different benchmarks are shown in Table 1 and Table 2.

Evaluation Procedure. We adopt a systematic procedure for evaluating the role-playing agents. The methodology includes the following components:

- **Dialogue Generation**: The agent is prompted to engage in both single-turn and multi-turn dialogues based on predefined scenarios, which are carefully designed to capture various aspects of the agent's role-playing ability.
- **Automated Scoring**: Each generated response is assessed by GPT-4o using the described evaluation metrics, with the evaluator providing a score for each metric on a scale from 1 (poor) to 5 (excellent).
- **Final Score Calculation**: For each benchmark (BaiJia and Character-LLM), the average scores across all metrics and all dialogues are calculated to provide a comprehensive assessment of the agent's performance.

Consistency of Human Evaluation. To evaluate the alignment between automated LLM evaluations and human judgments in character customization tasks, we compute Spearman's ρ and Kendall's τ rank correlation coefficients. We recruit 10 human annotators, each assigned two characters and asked to engage in at least 20-turn Chinese dialogues with LLM judge based on Deepseek-R1 [30]. Upon completion, annotators assign an overall quality score to each model on a

Table 2. Character-LLM Evaluation Metrics for Dialogue

Metric	Description
Personality	Measures the degree to which the agent consistently reflects the predefined character's personality across dialogues.
Values	Assesses the consistency of the agent's ethical, moral, or philosophical stances as aligned with the character profile.
Memorization	Evaluates the agent's ability to accurately recall past dialogue context and maintain coherent narrative continuity.
Hallucination	Determines the extent to which the agent produces factually inaccurate or fabricated responses.
Stability	Measures the consistency of agent responses when presented with similar or identical dialogue contexts across different interactions.

1-5 scale, which serves as the reference for human rankings. We then compare these human-derived rankings with automated LLM rankings across different character sets. The results show that both Spearman's ρ and Kendall's τ exceed 0.8, indicating a strong correlation between LLM-based and human evaluations. This confirms the reliability of our evaluation method in reflecting human judgment on character customization quality.

Table 3. Experimental results on BaiJia benchmark.

Models	CC	EI	DA	CR	CHA	CA	Avg
ChatGLM-6B	4.52	3.90	4.10	3.75	4.48	3.90	4.11
Qwen2.5-7B	4.63	4.12	4.32	4.09	4.70	4.22	4.35
LLaMA3-8B	4.50	3.92	4.00	3.78	4.34	3.91	4.08
Baichuan-NPC	4.45	3.83	4.00	3.70	3.85	4.05	3.98
Xingchen	4.26	3.73	3.94	3.52	4.29	3.72	3.91
SFT	4.91	4.17	4.69	4.16	4.71	4.26	4.48
SFT + Dynasty RM	4.71	4.21	4.52	4.25	4.65	4.58	4.49
SFT + Position RM	4.83	4.43	4.74	4.42	4.93	4.64	4.66
SFT + Regional RM	4.87	4.32	4.73	4.29	4.76	**4.73**	4.62
SFT + All Three RMs	**4.92**	**4.45**	**4.76**	4.43	**4.97**	4.68	**4.70**
SFT + DPO	4.89	4.43	4.78	**4.45**	4.92	4.66	4.69

4.3 Main Results

Comparisons between our method and baseline approaches on two benchmarks are presented in Table 3 and Table 4. Our AAPO model shows significant advan-

Table 4. Experimental results on the Character-LLM benchmark of Newton.

Models	Personality	Values	Memorization	Hallucination	Stability
GPT-3.5	4.5	3.9	4.1	3.7	4.5
Alpaca	4.2	4.0	4.1	3.5	4.3
Vicuna	4.8	4.1	4.5	3.7	4.6
Character-LLM	6.5	4.5	6.3	**6.7**	**6.6**
DPO	**6.7**	**4.9**	**6.5**	6.6	**6.6**

tages in all evaluation dimensions, validating the effectiveness of the multidimensional reward in PPO and DPO optimization.

Experiments on BaiJia Benchmark. Our AAPO model variants, demonstrated improved performance compared to many baselines. SFT + All Three RMs achieved the highest average score of 4.70. It also had the highest scores in multiple metrics, such as 4.92 in CC, 4.45 in EI, and 4.76 in DA, highlighting its overall superiority in handling different aspects of the tasks on this benchmark. SFT + Position RM also showed strong performance with an average score of 4.66, especially excelling in the DA metric with a score of 4.74.

Experiments on Character-LLM Benchmark. Our AAPO model, represented by DPO in this benchmark, outperformed the baselines significantly. DPO achieved the highest scores in Personality (6.7), Memorization (6.5), and had high scores in other metrics as well. It demonstrated strong overall performance, indicating its effectiveness in enhancing the model's capabilities in aspects such as personality expression, value assessment, and memorization on the Character-LLM benchmark of Newton.

Table 5. Hyper-parameter experiment results for different weight combinations

(a) BaiJia benchmark

α	β	γ	**Average**
0.2	0.5	0.3	4.67
0.3	0.4	0.3	**4.70**
0.4	0.3	0.3	4.68

(b) Character-LLM benchmark

α	β	γ	**Average**
0.3	0.3	0.4	4.65
0.25	0.45	0.3	4.69
0.2	0.3	0.5	**4.72**

4.4 Hyper-Parameter Analysis

To analyze the impact of different weight combinations of the three reward functions on the model's performance, we conducted a hyperparameter analysis. The results are presented in Table 5.

- For the BaiJia benchmark (Table 5(a)), when $\alpha = 0.3$, $\beta = 0.4$, and $\gamma = 0.3$, the model achieves an average score of 4.70, which is relatively high among the tested combinations. This indicates that in scenarios related to the Baijia benchmark, such a weight distribution can better balance the contributions of the three reward functions, enhancing the model's performance in maintaining character consistency and cultural alignment.
- For the Character-LLM benchmark (Table 5(b)), the combination $\alpha = 0.2$, $\beta = 0.3$, and $\gamma = 0.5$ yields an average score of 4.72, demonstrating superior performance. This suggests that in the context of the Character-LLM benchmark, increasing the weight of the third reward function (γ) can better adapt to diverse role-playing scenarios, improving the model's ability to maintain persona consistency and linguistic style.

Overall, the hyperparameter analysis reveals that different weight combinations of the three reward functions have distinct effects on the model's performance, and optimizing these weights according to the characteristics of the dataset can enhance the model's effectiveness in various role-playing tasks.

4.5 Ablation Study

To further evaluate the contribution of each reward model within the PPO-based complete architecture—composed of three weighted reward models (official position, dynasty, and region)—we conducted an ablation study by removing individual reward models while retaining PPO. The key findings are as follows:

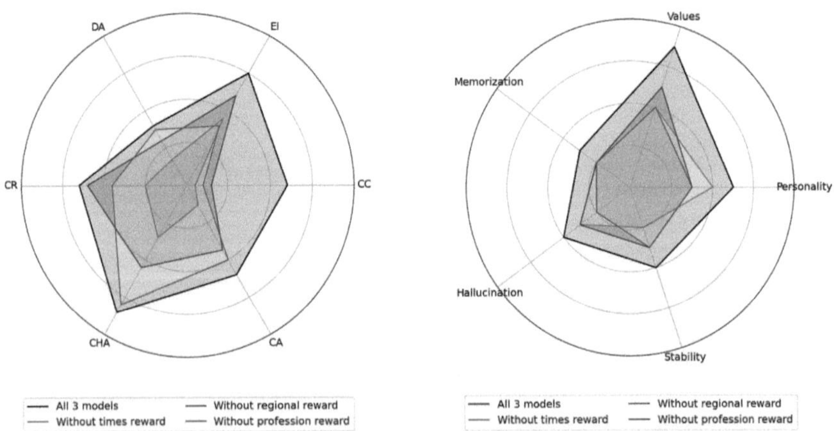

(a) BaiJia benchmark (b) Character-LLM benchmark

Fig. 2. Ablation studies on BaiJia and Character-LLM benchmarks. Comparison of our model's performance with different combination of reward models.

- **Without Official Position Reward Model**: As shown in Fig. 2(a), in official position-related dialogues of the BaiJia benchmark, the character consistency score dropped from 4.2 (full model) to 3.5 (on a 5-point scale). This demonstrates the critical role of the official position reward model in maintaining the identity consistency of historical roles, particularly in knowledge-dense scenarios involving hierarchical or positional attributes.
- **Without Dynasty Reward Model**: Observing Fig. 2(b), the historical accuracy index decreased by 8% in dynasty-related dialogues. This highlights the indispensable function of the dynasty reward model in cultural alignment, ensuring the model adheres to historical timelines, events, and background knowledge—core components of cross-temporal role-playing coherence.
- **Without Region Reward Model**: Experimental results show a 12% decline in linguistic style coherence within regional characteristic scenarios. This underscores the region reward model's contribution to adaptive scenario alignment, enabling the model to preserve appropriate dialectal features, idiomatic expressions, or cultural nuances specific to different geographical contexts.

These ablation results directly support the abstract's assertion that AAPO ensures attribute consistency through multidimensional signals, verifying that each reward model within the PPO framework is essential for handling distinct knowledge domains. The performance degradation observed when removing any single component highlights their synergistic role in maintaining robust cultural-linguistic alignment and scenario adaptability, thereby validating the design rationale of the multi-reward architecture.

5 Conclusion

In this paper, the Attribute-Aligned Policy Optimization (AAPO) framework, a reinforcement learning approach aimed at enhancing the alignment of role-playing agents with predefined character profiles, is presented. The framework offers training flexibility by integrating DPO or PPO to address distinct optimization objectives, and constructs preference data with SFT outputs as negative samples and GPT-4o-generated responses as positive samples to ensure high-quality training data. Extensive experiments on the BaiJia and Character-LLM benchmarks demonstrate that the AAPO framework consistently surpasses baseline models in maintaining character consistency, linguistic style, and cultural alignment, effectively adapting to diverse role-playing scenarios with robustness in high-knowledge contexts and coherence in low-knowledge settings. Analytical results reveal that DPO is particularly effective in optimizing explicit preference alignment, while PPO excels at multi-attribute optimization via weighted reward models, showcasing the dual approach's flexibility for different application scenarios and establishing AAPO as a versatile framework to enhance the performance of role-playing agents.

In future work, we plan to explore the integration of adaptive reward functions that dynamically adjust to user preferences, further enhancing the personalization of role-playing agents. In addition, our objective is to investigate the impact of larger-scale models and more complex character attributes on agent performance.

References

1. Chen, N., et al.: The Oscars of AI Theater: A Survey on Role-Playing with Language Models. In: arXiv preprint arXiv:2407.11484 (2024)
2. Dubey, A., et al.: The LLaMA 3 Herd of Models. In: arXiv preprint arXiv:2407.21783 (2024)
3. Tu, Q., et al.: CharacterEval: A Chinese Benchmark for Role-Playing Conversational Agent Evaluation. 2024. arXiv:2401.01275 [cs.CL]. https://arxiv.org/abs/2401.01275
4. Zhou, J., et al.: CharacterBench: benchmarking character customization of large language models. In: Proceedings of the AAAI Conference on Artificial Intelligence (AAAI). 2025. https://doi.org/10.48550/arXiv.2412.11912.arXiv:2412.11912 [cs.CL]
5. Chen, X., Sun, H., Liu, Y., et al.: MMRole: a comprehensive framework for developing and evaluating multimodal role - playing agents. In: arXiv preprint arXiv:2501.00345 (2025)
6. Wang, X., et al.: InCharacter: Evaluating Personality Fidelity in RolePlaying Agents through Psychological Interviews (2024). arXiv:2310.17976 [cs.CL]. url: https://arxiv.org/abs/2310.17976
7. Samuel, V., et al.: PersonaGym: evaluating persona agents and LLMs. https://arxiv.org/abs/2407.18416 (2024). arXiv:2407.18416 [cs.CL]
8. Wang, Z., et al.: RoleLLM: benchmarking, eliciting, and enhancing role-playing abilities of large language models. In: arXiv preprint arXiv:2310.00746 (2023)
9. Zhou, J., et al.: CharacterGLM: customizing chinese conversational AI characters with large language models. In: arXiv preprint arXiv:2311.16832 (2023)
10. Liu, J., Ni, Z., Que, H., et al.: RoleAgent: building, interacting, and benchmarking high-quality role-playing agents from scripts. In: Proceedings of the Conference on Innovative Applications of Artificial Intelligence (IAAI), pp. 123–134 (2024)
11. Shao, Y., et al.: Character-LLM: a trainable agent for role-playing. In: arXiv preprint arXiv:2310.04689 (2023)
12. Li, C., et al.: ChatHaruhi: reviving anime character in reality via large language model. In: arXiv preprint arXiv:2308.09597 (2023)
13. Zhang, Y., Sun, X., Li, L., et al.: Personalized dialogue agents with personality - constrained fine - tuning. In: Proceedings of the 2023 Conference on Empirical Methods in Natural Language Processing, pp. 567–578 (2023)
14. Ran, Y., Wang, X., Xu, R., et al.: Capturing minds, not just words: enhancing role - playing language models with personality - indicative data. In: arXiv preprint arXiv:2406.18921 (2024)
15. Yu, Y., et al.: BEYOND DIALOGUE: a profile-dialogue alignment framework towards general role-playing language model. In: arXiv preprint arXiv:2408.10903 (2024)
16. Rafailov, R., et al.: Direct preference optimization: your language model is secretly a reward model. In: arXiv preprint arXiv:2305.18290 (2023)
17. Schulman, J., et al.: Proximal Policy Optimization Algorithms. In: arXiv preprint arXiv:1707.06347 (2017)

18. Chen, J., et al.: Large language models meet harry potter: a dataset for aligning dialogue agents with characters. In: Findings of the Association for Computational Linguistics: EMNLP 2023 (2023)
19. Bai, T., et al.: BaiJia: an open role-playing platform of chinese historical characters. In: Proceedings of the 62nd Annual Meeting of the Association for Computational Linguistics. https://baijia.online and arXiv:2404.xxxxx (2024)
20. Urbanek, J., et al.: LIGHT: learning in interactive games with humans and text. In: arXiv preprint arXiv:1903.03094 (2019)
21. Tu, Q., et al.: CharacterEval: a Chinese benchmark for role-playing conversational agent evaluation. In: arXiv preprint arXiv:2401.01275 (2024)
22. Lu, K., et al.: DITTO: large language models are superpositions of all characters: attaining arbitrary role-play via self-alignment. In: arXiv preprint arXiv:2401.12474 (2024)
23. Ouyang, L., et al.: Training language models to follow instructions with human feedback. In: arXiv preprint arXiv:2203.02155 (2022)
24. Ziegler, D.M., et al.: Fine-Tuning Language Models from Human Preferences. In: arXiv preprint arXiv:1909.08593 (2019)
25. Bai, Y., et al.: Qwen Technical Report. In: arXiv preprint arXiv:2309.16609 (2023)
26. Qwen Team. Qwen2.5: A Party of Foundation Models. Sept. 2024. url: https://qwenlm.github.io/blog/qwen2.5/
27. Grattafiori, A., et al.: The Llama 3 Herd of Models. 2024. arXiv:2407. 21783 [cs.AI]. https://arxiv.org/abs/2407.21783
28. Baichuan. BaichuanNPC Website (2024). https://npc.baichuan-ai.com/. Accessed 12 July 2024
29. Alibaba Group. Tongyi Xingchen (2024). https://tongyi.aliyun.com/xingchen/. Accessed 12 June 2024
30. DeepSeek Team: DeepSeek - R1: Incentivizing Reasoning Capability in LLMs via Reinforcement Learning. In: arXiv preprint arXiv:2501.12948 (2025)

Medical Question-Physician Robustness Routing for Community Healthcare Services

Wenchao Sun[1], Zhengliang Shi[1], Pengjie Ren[1], Jun Ma[1], Zhaochun Ren[2], and Zhumin Chen[1(✉)]

[1] Shandong University, Qingdao, China
chenzhumin@sdu.edu.cn

[2] Leiden University, Leiden, The Netherlands

Abstract. An increasing number of studies have been proposed for community healthcare services (CHS) that connect users and physicians. Complex descriptions of diseases and symptoms make CHS difficult to match users' amateur questions with physicians. In this study, we propose the task of *question-physician routing* to address this issue by matching questions and physicians. Vocabulary gaps, nonreciprocal commutations, and limited user profiling information in CHS make question-physician routing a challenging research problem. To address the above challenges, we propose a new *question-routing* approach to match a physician with a given question, where we argue that the assistance of external medical knowledge helps to improve the performance of question-physician routing. Specifically, we propose a medical question-routing framework, namely *deep medical question routing* (DMQR), which integrates external medical knowledge into the routing process. DMQR can be divided into three main components: First, we construct a medical knowledge extractor to extract knowledge from a medical knowledge base constructed based on external knowledge resources. Then, we propose a knowledge interpreter to integrate medical knowledge into the given question for a better representation. Lastly, we route top-k relevant candidate physicians to the question by employing a hierarchical multi-label classifier. To further enhance the robustness and efficiency of question-physician routing, we propose a virtual adversarial medical question routing optimization method, v-DMQR, and an efficient optimization way that uses anchor question-physician pairs, namely av-DMQR. Since there is no existing data in the literature, we collect a large-scale dataset from real-world CHS scenarios. Extensive experiments performed on our dataset verify the effectiveness of our proposed approach. Moreover, we find that our proposed approach significantly outperforms state-of-the-art baselines on medical question routing in terms of Recall, MAP, and MRR metrics.

Keywords: Community healthcare service · medical question routing · knowledge matching

Z. Li et al. (Eds.): CCIR 2025, LNCS 16369, pp. 26–48, 2026.
https://doi.org/10.1007/978-981-95-5637-3_3

1 Introduction

Recently, with more and more medical questions from patients to physicians, community healthcare services (CHS) have attracted considerable attention. Patients often ask medical questions with symptom descriptions and aim to obtain diagnoses from physicians. Therefore, helping patients to find a proper physician is becoming the key to CHS. To investigate proper connections between questions and physicians, in this study, we focus on the *question-physician routing* (QpR) problem w.r.t., CHS, i.e., matching medical questions with appropriate physicians. Intuitively, the procedure of QpR is complicated as professional medical terminologies exist in questions and physician descriptions, making diseases and symptoms difficult to be described by amateur users [40].

Many studies have established connections between questions and answers based on semantic relevance [35,41,50,52]. However, three challenges still exist that hinder these approaches in QpR: (1) vocabulary gap between questions and physicians; (2) nonreciprocal commutations; and (3) limited user profiling information. First, most patients lack professional knowledge in medical domains, resulting in the vocabulary gap problem between questions and physicians' features. Medical concepts in CHS expressed by patients and professional physicians are usually different. For example, "breathing difficulties" and "breathless" may be used by different patients to describe their symptom, but these two words refers to the same medical concept "dyspnea". Second, it is difficult to model reciprocal information commutation between questions and physicians in QpR. In CHS, the roles of askers (patients) and answerers (physicians) are not exchangeable. Third, most patients are extremely rare to share profiling information for privacy reasons, making it challenging to find proper physicians.

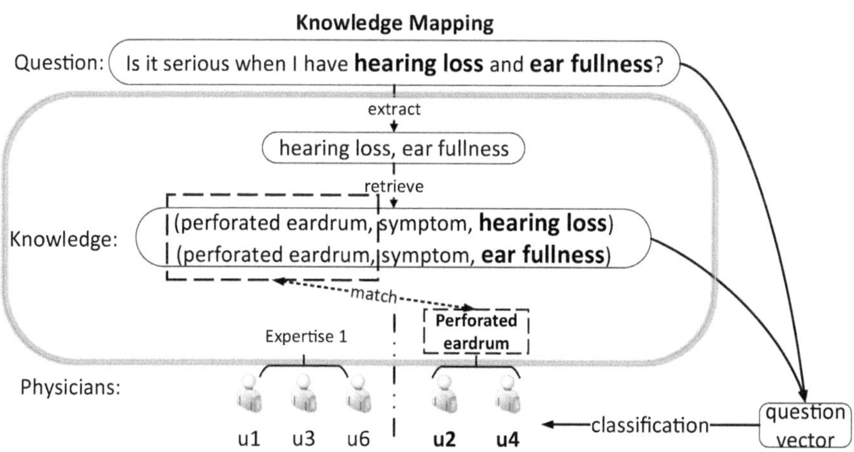

Fig. 1. An overview of our proposed knowledge mapping mechanism.

To address the above challenges, we consider incorporating medical knowledge into QpR procedure using a knowledge-based mapping mechanism. As illustrated in Fig. 1, we intend to connects the question and physicians through a knowledge-aware mapping component with semantic triples. For each semantic triple, the tailed entity refers to the symptoms of the patient (e.g., "hearing loss" and "ear fullness"), whereas the head entity refers to the disease (e.g., "perforated eardrum"). Unlike regular mapping approaches in the previous question routing studies [50,54], our strategy focuses on knowledge-level question-physician matching, which generates tremendous medical facts. Additionally, exhaustive relations between questions and physicians are provided through the procedure.

Specifically, we propose a novel neural question routing framework, namely deep medical question routing (DMQR), which uses medical knowledge to construct knowledge level question-physician matching. We first construct a medical knowledge extractor to extract knowledge from medical knowledge base. By proposing to integrate medical knowledge into questions, we transfer QpR into a multi-label classification problem where each physician is considered as a label. Several machine learning models are vulnerable to adversarial data [47]. To further enhance the robustness and efficiency of QpR, we propose a virtual adversarial medical question routing algorithm, v-DMQR, and an efficient version that uses anchor question-physician pairs, namely av-DMQR. Our virtual adversarial question routing algorithm generates a virtual adversarial representation for each original physician. Then, we regularize the model so that it generates the same output distribution as that produced by an adversarial perturbation of the physician.

We performed our experiments on a large-scale real-world dataset. Extensive results verify that our approach outperforms all of the baselines in terms of Recall, MAP, and MRR metrics. We also verified that v-DMQR and av-DMQR enhance the robustness of the virtual adversarial representation of physicians and the generalization performance for original question-physician pairs.

Our primary contributions can be summarized as follows:

- We propose the task of question-physician routing in community healthcare services.
- We develop a knowledge mapping mechanism between questions and physicians through handling complicated relationships among different diseases and symptoms.
- We propose a deep medical question routing framework, which consists of a medical knowledge extractor, a knowledge graph embedding module, and a knowledge interpreter.
- We propose two virtual adversarial learning algorithms to enhance the robustness and efficiency of DMQR: v-DMQR and av-DMQR.
- We collect a new real-world dataset. Our experimental results verify that our approaches outperform all baselines.

The rest of this study is organized as follows. Section 2 introduces related works. Section 3 explains the question routing problem in our work. Section 4 describes our approach. Section 5 and Sect. 6 details the experimental setups, results and analysis. Section 7 concludes this study and discusses future work.

2 Related Work

In this section, we show related work about question routing. Existing studies on question routing can be categorized into 2 classes: structure-based question routing and learning-based question routing.

Without using textual information, structure-based question routing approaches use link analysis in the routing procedure [9,10,19,22,27,39,40,46, 50,55]. [52,54] developed a user network from a question-answering service to identify users. Similarly, [11] capture the communication patterns through a graph of message exchanges. [33] used a graph to represent the academic co-authorship network. [42] proposed to use multiple topics to reflect users' interests by computing cosine similarities between users and questions. Although great success has been achieved by these approaches, existing structure-based question routing approaches hold limitations when applied to QpR due to the lack of textual information, which often includes crucial information, e.g., symptoms, medications, and treatments.

Learning-based question routing strategies focus on using textual information in questions [1–5,7,13,17,18,20,22,25,29–32,34–36,38,40,45,49,51,56]. Early studies on learning-based question routing usually construct user profiles by gathering users' personal information or previously answered questions. [43] selected the top-k users according to the similarity between the given question and user profiles. [42] proposed a model using multiple topics to reflect interests and route questions to users according to their interests. Similarly, [21] introduced a topic-level model to build up user profiles. [53] utilized tensor model and topic model simultaneously to extract latent semantic relations among asker, question and answerer. [35] applied the knowledge graph embedding model to integrate structure and topic features into a unified framework for question routing in CQA sites. However, this study does not employ deep learning approaches. Most crucially, they construct triples by filtering the raw CQA data rather than employing the professional knowledge directly written by experts. Although these approaches are effective in enhancing routing performance, limitations still exist regarding the question representations. Recently, neural question routing approaches apply deep neural networks to represent questions and user profiling information [2,3,7,45]. [3] proposed a deep neural network to extract semantic features from questions and users' profiles. However, limitations still exist when we apply these learning-based studies combining textual information to QpR, as most of them neglect external medical knowledge.

3 Problem Formulation

In this section, we provide notions and key concepts of our research problem. We first list the glossary in Table 1.

Table 1. glossary.

Symbol	Description
Q	*questions set*
q_n	*n-th question,* $q_n \in Q$
$\mathcal{V}$	*the vocabulary*
w_i	*a word in question* q_n, $w_i \in V$
MTD	*medical terminology dictionary*
mt_i	*a medical terminology,* $mt_i \in MTD$
$\boldsymbol{q_n}$	*representation of* q_n
q_n'	*a new sequence that replaces* w_i with mt_i
$\boldsymbol{q_n'}$	*representation of* q_n'
$\boldsymbol{R_{q_n}}$	*the united question representation,* $\boldsymbol{R_{q_n}} = [\mathbf{q_n}, \mathbf{q_n'}]^T$
UP	*physicians set*
u_i	*a physician,* $u_i \in UP$
E	*entities set*
h,t	*head entity and tail entity,* $h \in E$, $t \in E$
R	*relations set*
r	*relation between* h *and* t, $r \in R$
S,S'	*triples set and negative sample of* S, *respectively*
(h, r, t)	*a triple,* $(h, r, t) \in S$
$\boldsymbol{l_h}$,$\boldsymbol{l_r}$,$\boldsymbol{l_t}$	*representation of* h,r,t
q_n^{mt}	*a list of medical terminologies,* q_n^{mt}: $(mt_1, mt_2, \ldots, mt_x)$
$d(h + r)$	*the dissimilarity between* $h + r$ and t
x_t	*the element of* q *and* q'
D_ϕ	*the discriminative model with parameter* ϕ
G_θ	*the generative model with parameter* θ
$p_{GT}(u\|q_n)$	*ground-truth distribution of physicians over n-th question*
$p_\phi(r\|u_i, q_n)$	*probability of candidate* u_i *having or not having expertise on question* q_n
D_{ϕ^*}	*the optimal discriminative model*
G_{θ^*}	*the optimal generative model*
S	*word sequences set*
s_n	*n-th word sequence,* $s_n \in S$
$\boldsymbol{u_i^\phi}$,$\boldsymbol{u_i^\theta}$	u_i*'s representation*
$\boldsymbol{w_j^\phi}$,$\boldsymbol{w_j^\theta}$	w_j*'s representation*
$\mathcal{D}$	*document set*
d_k	*a document,* $d_k \in \mathcal{D}$
$p_{\widetilde{GT}}(u_i\|d_k)$	*pseudo ground-truth distribution of* u_i *over* d_k
M_{d_k}	*m-grams set extracted from* d_k
$d_k^{(l)}$	*l-th m-grams,* $d_k^{(l)} \in M_{d_k}$
U_{d_k}	*set of physicians associated with* d_k

Given a set of questions Q, we denote each question as $q_n \in Q$, the representation of q_n as $\boldsymbol{R}_{q_n} = [\mathbf{q_n}, \mathbf{q'_n}]^T$, and the set of all physicians as UP. We aim to identify a list of physicians $\{u_1, u_2, \ldots, u_k\}$, $u_i \in UP$. The list UL contains the top k most suitable physicians to answer q_n. In our study, we set the problem of question routing as a multi-label classification task, where the number of all physicians, i.e., $|UP|$, is the total number of classes. We denote the probability of a physician u_i to answer a question q_n as $p(u_i|q_n)$. Then we compute the probability using a softmax function [37], so we have:

$$p(u_i|q_n) = \frac{e^{\delta*(W_i*\boldsymbol{R}_{q_n}+b_i)}}{\sum_{j=1}^{|U|} e^{\delta*(W_j*\boldsymbol{R}_{q_n}+b_j)}}, \tag{1}$$

where W_i and b_i represent the parameters of a fully connected layer, and δ is the parameter of softmax function.

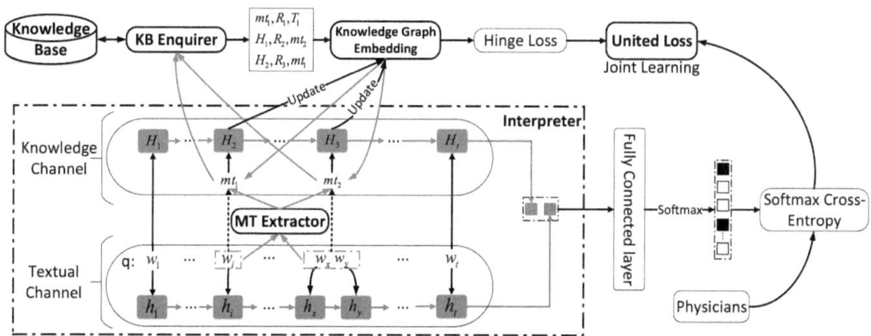

Fig. 2. The framework of our model. It consists of three components: the medical knowledge extractor, the knowledge graph embedding module, and the knowledge interpreter.

4 Model

In this section, we first present an overview of our proposed model. Then, we detail each component in our model and two virtual adversarial learning algorithms.

4.1 Overview

The framework of the deep medical question routing (DMQR) model is illustrated in Fig. 2. In general, DMQR consists of three components: the medical knowledge extractor, the knowledge graph embedding module, and the knowledge interpreter. The basic idea of DMQR is to develop a hidden representation of the given question, and then generate predictions based on it.

In the beginning, the medical knowledge extractor extracts medical terminologies from the input question sequence q_n. In the knowledge interpreter component, we establish two channels to model the question with two types of representations: the textual and knowledge channels. For the textual channel, q_n is denoted as a word sequence q_n: $(w_1, w_2, \ldots, w_m)$ where w_i represents a word. For the knowledge channel, the list of medical terminologies recognized from q_n is denoted as $(mt_1, mt_2, \ldots, mt_x)$ where mt_i represents a medical terminology. We replace w_i by mt_j, and construct a new sequence q_n': $(\ldots, w_i, \ldots, mt_j, \ldots)$. For q_n and q_n', we use two LSTMs to generate the corresponding representation, and then we concatenate these two representations into a single question representation. After that, this single question representation is fed into a fully-connected layer to generate a ranking list over all physicians by a softmax function. Given the list of medical terminologies $(mt_1, mt_2, \ldots, mt_x)$, we employ the medical knowledge extractor to retrieve corresponding triples from a knowledge base, then these triples are fed to the knowledge graph embedding module to generate representations of medical terminologies. Finally, we route top-k relevant candidate physicians to the question by employing a multi-label classifier. In the training process, the medical terminology representation is updated by the knowledge graph embedding module and the knowledge interpreter. In the following part of this section, we detail each component of the DMQR.

4.2 Medical Knowledge Extractor

The medical knowledge extractor consists of three parts: the medical knowledge base(KB), the medical terminology(MT) extractor and the knowledge base enquirer. We collect data from HealthTap[1] and extract triples from these data to construct a medical KB. In this KB, an item of knowledge is denoted as a triple (h, r, t), where h, t, and r represent the head entity, tail entity, and the relation between them respectively. In all triples, both h and t are medical terminologies, which is a type of phrase employed to precisely describe the health conditions such as symptoms, and medicines. We designed an extractor to extract MT from questions, and an MT can be either a head entity or a tail entity. The key operation of this module is to recognize a named entity, which has various approaches. Based on the MT dictionary, we use a maximum matching algorithm to recognize medical terminologies from questions. The output of the MT extractor is a list q_n^{mt}: $(mt_1, mt_2, \ldots, mt_x)$, which will be taken as the input of the KB enquirer. With q_n^{mt}, KB enquirer retrieves corresponding triples from KB. If the input medical terminology matches one of the head and tail entities in a triple, this triple will be retrieved as one output of the KB enquirer. The output list of triples is shown in Fig. 1. These triples are then taken as the input for the next module.

[1] www.healthtap.com.

4.3 Knowledge Graph Embedding

We learn the representations of entities and relations using TransE [8], which interprets the relationship as the translation operation between head and tail entities. Given a triple fact $(h, r, t) \in S$, h and $t \in E$, $r \in R$, S is the set of all triples in KB, E and R represent the set of entities and relations. We use $d(h + r, t)$ to estimate the difference between $h + r$ and t, the margin-based objective function is minimized as follows,

$$L1 = \sum_{(h,r,t) \in S} \sum_{(h',r,t') \in S'} \max(0, \gamma + d(h + r, t) - d(h' + r, t')), \tag{2}$$

$$S' = \{(h', r, t) | h' \in E\} \cup \{(h, r, t') | t' \in E\}. \tag{3}$$

In this equation, γ is a margin hyper-parameter. The negative sample of S is represented as S', in which one of the head and tail entities is randomly replaced by another entity that has no relation to the original entity in the knowledge base.

In our study, for each positive training triple, we randomly sample four negative triples from S'. If the medical terminology recognized from the question is on the head position of the training triple, we randomly replace the tail entity in the training triple to generate a new triple. Additionally, we regard it as a negative triple if and only if it does not belong to the training triples.

4.4 Knowledge Interpreter

For a given question q_n, we design two channels, the textual channel and the knowledge channel, to model the question with two types of representations. For the textual channel, we denote q_n as a word sequence $(w_1, w_2, w_3, \ldots, w_m)$, where w_i represents a word. The list of medical terminologies recognized from q_n is denoted as q_n^{mt}: $(mt_1, mt_2, \ldots, mt_x)$ where mt_i represents a medical terminology. For the knowledge channel, we replace w_i by mt_j, and construct a new sequence q'_n: $(\ldots, w_i, \ldots, mt_j, \ldots)$.

For q_n and q'_n, we employ a Long Short-Term Memory(LSTM) described in Sect. 4.4 to generate the textual representations $\boldsymbol{q_n}$ and $\boldsymbol{q'_n}$. Then, we concatenate $\boldsymbol{q_n}$ and $\boldsymbol{q'_n}$ into a single question representation $\boldsymbol{R_{q_n}} = [\mathbf{q_n}, \mathbf{q'_n}]^T$ to integrate knowledge into the question representation.

We design our knowledge interpreter based on the Long Short-Term Memory (LSTM) ([24]). We use two LSTMs to encode the textual information and knowledge information of the question into two different representations respectively. By concatenating the representations of $\boldsymbol{q_n}$ and $\boldsymbol{q'_n}$ described in Sect. 3, we obtain the question representation $\boldsymbol{R_{q_n}} = [\mathbf{q_n}, \mathbf{q'_n}]^T$.

By integrating medical knowledge into questions, we transfer DMQR into a multi-label classification problem where each physician is considered as a label. After we obtain the question representation, we map it to a length-K vector of values using the softmax function, where K represents the number of classes corresponding to the number of candidate physicians. The i-th value of this vector represents the probability that the i-th physician is selected to be the answerer of the question.

4.5 Optimization

In this section, we first describe the optimization of DMQR with a joint loss function, then we demonstrate two adversarial algorithms based on the joint loss function. To further enhance the robustness of question-physician routing, we propose a virtual adversarial medical question routing algorithm, namely v-DMQR. To improve the efficiency, we propose the av-DMQR algorithm with anchor question-physician pairs.

DMQR. For question vector $R_{q_n} = [\mathbf{q_n}, \mathbf{q'_n}]^T$, we calculate the probability of candidate physician u_i being the correct answerer of question q_n, given the question sequence and medical terminologies contained in the question. This probability is

$$P(u_i|q_n, E) = \sigma(W[\mathbf{q_n}, \mathbf{q'_n}]^T + b), \tag{4}$$

where q_n reprensents the question, E is the set of recognized medical terminologies contained in the question, σ represents the softmax function, W and b are the weight and bias respectively.

Specifically, given R_{q_n}:$(r_1, r_2, \ldots, r_n)$ where r_i represents an element of R_{q_n}, it is taken as the input of a fully-connected layer. Then, we use the softmax cross entropy function to be the object function of the classification task.

By adding Eqs. 2 and the above softmax cross entropy function, we obtain the final object function (5),

$$\begin{aligned} L = \alpha * L1 + \beta * L2 = &\alpha * \sum_{(h,r,t)\in S} \sum_{(h',r,t')\in S'} \max(0, \gamma + d(h+r,t) - d(h'+r,t'))+ \\ &\beta * -\frac{1}{n}\sum[y\ln(a) + (1-y)\ln(1-a)], \end{aligned} \tag{5}$$

where

$$S' = \{(h', r, t)|h' \in E\} \cup \{(h, r, t')|t' \in E\}. \tag{6}$$

n represents the number of training samples, y is the true label vector, and a is the output vector of softmax function. We set α and β both to 1, and we find that the performance of our model has no significant change when we modify α and β.

V-DMQR. Our proposed v-DMQR algorithm is a minimax two-player game that consists of a discriminative model D_ϕ with parameter ϕ and a generative model G_θ with parameter θ. The generative model would try generating (in our task, select) relevant physicians to the question which looks like the ground-truth relevant physician and thus could fool the discriminative model. In this study, we regard the DMQR model as the generative model G_θ, which can predict the probability of a physician u_i to answer question q as $p_\theta(u_i|q_n)$ in

Eq. 1. The discriminative model tries to capture a clear distinction between the ground-truth physicians and the generated ones made by its opponent generative model. Competition in this game drives our algorithm to enhance the robustness of the representation of physicians and generalization performance for original question-physician pairs.

Suppose we have N questions, D_ϕ and G_θ play the following two-player minimax game with value function $J^{G_{\theta*},D_{\phi*}}$:

$$J^{G_{\theta*},D_{\phi*}} = \min_\theta \max_\phi \sum_{n=1}^{N} (\mathbb{E}_{u\sim p_{GT}(u|q_n)}[\log D_\phi(u|q_n)] + \mathbb{E}_{u\sim p_\theta(u|q_n)}[\log(1 - D_\phi(u|q_n))]), \tag{7}$$

where u is a candidate physician, $p_{GT}(u|q_n)$ is the ground-truth distribution of physicians to the n-th question q_n. In Eq. 7, the generator G_θ is represented as $p_\theta(u|q_n)$ which defined in Eq. 1, and the $D_\phi(u_i|q_n)$ is defined as

$$D_\phi(u_i|q_n) = p_\phi(r = 1|u_i, q_n)^{r_{in}} p_\phi(r = 0|u_i, q_n)^{r_{1-in}}. \tag{8}$$

In Eq. 8, $p_\phi(r = 1|u_i, q_n$ and $p_\phi(r = 0|u_i, q_n)$ are the ground-truth probabilities of candidate u_i respectively, which can be obtained by the distribution $p_{GT}(u|q)$. $r_{in} = 1$ indicates physician u_i have expertise on question q_n and vice versa.

Av-DMQR. Considering the ground-truth distribution $p_{GT}(u|q_n)$ is not always available, the optimal discriminative model and generative model G_{θ^*} cannot be obtained using Eq. 7. So We propose an efficient unsupervised version of v-DMQR, namely av-DMQR..

We transfer Eq. 7 to the unsupervised two-player minimax game as the following:

$$J^{G_{\theta*},D_{\phi*}} = \min_\theta \max_\phi \sum_{n=1}^{|S|} (\mathbb{E}_{u\sim p_\phi(u|s_n)}[\log D_\phi(u|s_n)] + \mathbb{E}_{u\sim p_\theta(u|s_n)}[\log(1 - D_\phi(u|s_n))]), \tag{9}$$

where $S = \{s_n\}_{n=1}^{|S|}$ is a set of word sequences, and a question can be regarded as a word sequence as well. All questions are extracted from documents in $\mathcal{D}$, $s_n = w_1, ..., w_{|s_n|}$ is the n-th word sequence, w_i is a word from a vocabulary $\mathcal{V}$, $|s_n|$ and $|S|$ is the size of the n-th sequence and the total number of word sequences in set S, respectively. The set of word sequences S can be obtained in an unsupervised way, and we can model each sequence as m-grams extracted from documents.

Next we define $p_\phi(u_i|s_n)$, $p_\theta(u_i|s_n)$ and D_ϕ in Eq. 9 via an unsupervised way. $p_\phi(u_i|s_n)$ is defined as:

$$p_\phi(u_i|s_n) \overset{rank}{=} \frac{1}{Z_1} \exp\left(\sum_{j=1}^{|s_n|} \log(p_\phi(u_i|w_j))\right), \tag{10}$$

where $\tilde{p}_\phi(u_i|w_1, ..., w_{|s_n|})$ reprensents the unnormalized score,

$$Z_1 = \sum_{i=1}^{|UP|} \exp\left(\sum_{j=1}^{|s_n|} \log(p_\phi(u_i|w_j))\right) \tag{11}$$

is a normalization term. $\stackrel{rank}{=}$ means that ranking is equivalent between the former and latter equation. Additionally,

$$p_\phi(u_i|w_j) = \frac{1}{Z_2} \exp\left(\boldsymbol{u}_i^\phi \cdot (\boldsymbol{w}_j^\phi)^T + b_i^\phi\right), \tag{12}$$

where $\boldsymbol{u}_i^\phi$ and $\boldsymbol{w}_j^\phi$ represent the physician u_i's and the word w_j's semantic representation vectors respectively, b_i^ϕ is a bias parameter for candidate physician u_i, and $Z_2 = \sum_{i=1}^{|UP|} \exp\left(\boldsymbol{u}_i^\phi \cdot (\boldsymbol{w}_j^\phi)^T + b_i\right)$. On the whole, the parameter ϕ consists of $\{\boldsymbol{u}_i^\phi\}_{i=1}^{|UP|}$, the representations of all the candidate physicians, $\{\boldsymbol{w}_j^\phi\}_{j=1}^{|V|}$, the representations of all the words, and the corresponding biases $\{b_i^\phi\}_{i=1}^{|UP|}$, i.e., $\boldsymbol{\phi} = \{\{\boldsymbol{u}_i^\phi\}_{i=1}^{|UP|}, \{\boldsymbol{w}_j^\phi\}_{j=1}^{|V|}, \{b_i^\phi\}_{i=1}^{|UP|}\}$.

$p_\theta(u_i|s_n)$ in our generative model G_θ is defined as the same as in our discriminative model D_ϕ via Eqs. 10 and 12. Then, parameter θ in our generative model G_θ is $\boldsymbol{\theta} = \{\{\boldsymbol{u}_i^\theta\}_{i=1}^{|UP|}, \{\boldsymbol{w}_j^\theta\}_{j=1}^{|V|}, \{b_i^\theta\}_{i=1}^{|UP|}\}$.

Before the definition of D_θ, we first construct a pseudo ground-truth probability of candidate physician u_i having expertise on a document $d_k \in \mathcal{D}$, $p_{\widetilde{GT}}(u_i|d_k)$. The definition of $p_{\widetilde{GT}}(u_i|d_k)$ is:

$$p_{\widetilde{GT}}(u_i|d_k) = \begin{cases} 0, & u_i \notin U_{d_k}, \\ \frac{1}{|U_{d_k}|}, & u_i \in U_{d_k}, \end{cases} \tag{13}$$

where U_{d_k} and $|U_{d_k}|$ are a set of candidate physicians whose names or email addresses are observed in document d_k and the total number of all candidate physicians in the document d_k respectively. For each document $d \in \mathcal{D}$, we extract a set of m-grams and let M_{d_k} represent the set of m-grams extracted from d_k, let $d_k^{(l)} \in M_{d_k}$ represent the l-th m-grams. $\boldsymbol{p}_{\widetilde{GT}}(u_i|d_k) = \{p_{\widetilde{GT}}(u_i|d_k^{(l)})\}_{l=1}^{|M_{d_k}|}$, where $|M_{d_k}|$ represents the size of m-grams set extracted from d_k, and $p_{\widetilde{GT}}(u_i|d_k^{(l)}) = p_{\widetilde{GT}}(u_i|d_k)$ which can be obtained by Eq. 13. We also denote $\boldsymbol{p}_\phi(u_i|d_k)$ to be $\boldsymbol{p}_\phi(u_i|d_k) = \{p_\phi(u_i|d_k^{(l)})\}_{l=1}^{|M_{d_k}|}$. Here $p_\phi(u_i|d_k^{(l)}) = p_\phi(u_i|w_1^{d_k^{(l)}}, ..., w_m^{d_k^{(l)}})$ can be obtained by Eq. 10, and $w_x^{d_k^{(l)}}$ is the x-th word in the m-gram $d_k^{(l)}$.

Therefore, we define the discriminative model $D_\phi(u_i|d_k)$ based on the cross-entropy $C(\boldsymbol{p}_{\widetilde{GT}}(u_i|d_k), \boldsymbol{p}_\phi(u_i|d_k))$ as:

$$\begin{aligned} D_\phi(u_i|d_k) = &-\frac{|d_{max}|}{Z_3 \cdot |d_k| \cdot |M_{d_k}|} \sum_{l=1}^{|M_{d_k}|} \left(p_{\widetilde{GT}}(u_i|d_k^{(l)}) \cdot \log p_\phi(u_i|d_k^{(l)})\right) \\ &+\epsilon\left(\| \boldsymbol{u}_i^\phi \|_2^2 + \frac{1}{|M_{d_k}|} \sum_{j=1}^{|M_{d_k}|} \| \boldsymbol{w}_j^\phi \|_2^2\right), \end{aligned} \tag{14}$$

where $\| x \|_2$ represents the 2-norm of a vector x, ϵ represents a regularization parameter, $d_{max} = \arg\max_{d \in \mathcal{D}} |d|$ is the longest document, Z_3 is a normalization constant that forces $D_\phi(u|d)$ to be within the range(0,1), $|d_{max}|$ and $|d_k|$ are the length of the corresponding documents respectively.

In this study, we employ our supervised DMQR model as the generative model G_θ and $p(u_i|q_n)$ defined in Eq. 1 as $p_\theta(u_i|q_n)$, but our proposed unsupervised adversarial learning algorithm av-DMQR is possible under unsupervised circumstances.

The objective of the discriminative model is to maximize the log-likelihood of correctly distinguishing the candidate physicians from $p_\phi(u|s)$ and those generated from $p_\theta(u|s)$. We can obtain the optimal parameters for the discriminative model by maximizing Eq. 14 as:

$$\begin{aligned}\boldsymbol{\phi}^* = \arg\max_{\phi} \sum_{k=1}^{|\mathcal{D}|} (\frac{1}{|UP|} \sum_{i=1}^{|UP|} \log D_\phi(u_i|d_k) + \\ \mathbb{E}_{u \sim p_\theta(u|d_k)}[\log(1 - D_\phi(u|d_k))]).\end{aligned} \tag{15}$$

After we obtain the optimal parameter $\boldsymbol{\phi}^*$, we can optimize the generative model G_θ as:

$$\boldsymbol{\theta}^* = \arg\min_{\theta} \sum_{k=1}^{|\mathcal{D}|} \mathbb{E}_{u \sim p_\theta(u|d_k)}[\log(1 - D_\phi(u|d_k))]. \tag{16}$$

In Eq. 16, the sampling $u \sim p_\theta(u|d_k)$ is discrete, which is different from most GAN-based algorithms, thus, we employ policy gradient based reinforcement learning to obtain the optimal $\boldsymbol{\theta}^*$.

5 Experimental Setups

Before detailing our experimental setups, we first list research questions to guide our experiments:

- **RQ1**: Does our approach DMQR outperform the state-of-art question routing approaches?
- **RQ2**: Will the performance of our approach DMQR be affected if the data contain a low percentage of knowledge?
- **RQ3**: Is our knowledge mapping mechanism more helpful than the attention mechanism?

Finally, we make a case study to examine several effective and noneffective cases for our approach DMQR.

Table 2. Statistics of HealthTap dataset. The symbols # and $\#^c$ denote the number and the number of categories, respectively.

#Question	$\#^c$ MT	$\#^c$ Relation	$\#^c$ Triple	$\#^c$ Physician
233867	*5200*	*18*	*131182*	*737*

5.1 Dataset

We conduct our experiments and analyses on a real word dataset collected from HealthTap[2]. This dataset consists of semi-structured medical knowledge revised by professional physicians, and around 200 thousand answered questions. We develop the medical KB based on these semi-structured data and build the MT dictionary. Statistics of our dataset is shown in Table 2, including the number of questions and physicians, the number of types of MT, relation, and triple. This dataset will be released to public.

5.2 Implementation Details

We set γ in Eqs. 2 and 5 to 1, which is the margin hyper-parameter. We randomly initialize our model parameters using Xavier initialization to adjust the scale of initialization based on the number of input and output neurons. All of the parameters are initialized from a distribution with zero mean and variance. During training, we randomly sample four negative triples for each positive triple in each epoch. And we set the α and β in Eq. 5 both to 1. We set the hidden size of LSTM to 512,and the embedding size to 50 which is also initialized using Xavier initialization. To prevent overfitting, we apply the dropout approach, in which the keep probability of the neural network unit is set to 0.6 during the training process. The batch size is set to 512, and the learning rate employed in Adaptive Moment Estimation(Adam) optimization is set to 0.001. During adversarial learning, we set the sample number of generated candidate physicians to 20, and the length of m-grams of av-DMQR to 1. First, we pre-train our DMQR, then iteratively let the generative model and discriminative model performs the minimax game which updates the parameter ϕ and θ at each iteration until convergence.

5.3 Evaluation Metrics

For each question, the ground-truth gt is a set of physicians which have answered this question previously. Each of the physicians is denoted as an ID number from 0 to 736, and there are 737 physicians in total. First, we generate a list of 737 probabilities with each index corresponding to a physician. Then we sort the indexes from biggest to smallest according to the values of probabilities. Finally, we select the ID numbers of the top 20 physicians as the routing list, and we

[2] www.healthtap.com.

denote it as tp. For the convenience of evaluation, we generate an indicator list rsl with size 20 for each question. If a physician's ID number existing in tp is also contained in ground-truth gt, the corresponding position in rsl is assigned the value 1, 0 otherwise.

To access the performance of ranked lists, we adopt Recall [48,57], Mean Average Precision(MAP) [14] and Mean Reciprocal Rank(MRR) [12,16].

5.4 Baselines

Considering the lack of research in QRHC, we just consider two types of baselines in our experiments: typical baselines and deep learning baselines. Typical baselines are listed as follows.

- Support Vector Machine(SVM): This baseline is a quite representative approach of most machine learning approaches. It is a supervised learning model widely employed for classification or regression [23]. In this experiment, we extract unigram and bigram features from a question, and use a multi-label SVM to classify the different questions.
- Language Model(LM): This approach is commonly employed in expert finding [6]. It estimates a language model for each expert, and then rank experts by computing the question sentence probability according to the estimated language model. In this experiment, we employ the bigram language model and Laplace Smoothing method [15].

Due to the lack of physician interaction information in our dataset, the link analysis techniques [9] are unsuitable for our question routing scenario. Additionally, deep learning baselines are listed as follows.

- Question Routing using Deep Semantic Similarity Model(QR-DSSM): This approach first constructs physician profiles , then extracts semantic similarity features from questions and user profiles, and employs the features to rank user profiles [3]. This study does not share its code, so we re-implement this baseline in our experiment.
- Long Short-Term Memory(LSTM): This approach is a typical deep learning technique widely employed in processing sequence-related tasks [24]. Considering the characteristic of our task, we take this approach as a baseline model.
- Attention-based LSTM(Att-LSTM): This approach is a modified LSTM based on attention mechanism [44]. This method makes the generated question representation pay more attention on the key parts of the question sequence.
- BERT(Bidirectional Encoder Representations from Transformers): a groundbreaking natural language processing (NLP) model introduced by Google [28].
- Qwen2.5-instruct(0.5b/1.5b): a versatile large language model (LLM) series supporting both natural language understanding and generation [26].

6 Experimental Results

6.1 Performance Comparisons (RQ1)

Table 3 demonstrates the performance comparison of top-20 physician routing for SVM, LM, QR-DSSM, LSTM, Att-LSTM, DMQR, v-DMQR and av-DMQR. And DMQR outperforms all the other five baselines and achieves the best performance on Recall, MAP and MRR metrics. First, by introducing medical knowledge into question routing, our approach DMQR outperforms LSTM by 1.4% in terms of Recall, 1.4% in terms of MAP and 1.5% in terms of MRR metric. This shows that knowledge mapping is quite helpful for enhancing the accuracy of routing the suitable physician to the patient's question. Because MT contained in question usually conveys substantial information about diseases and symptoms.

Table 3. Performances comparison of top-20 physician routing for our method and other baselines. DIS and GEN mean discriminator model and generator model of v-DMQR and av-DMQR correspondingly.

Evaluation Metrics		Recall@20	MAP@20	MRR@20
SVM		*0.296*	*0.136*	*0.141*
LM		*0.311*	*0.149*	*0.156*
QR-DSSM		*0.311*	*0.142*	*0.155*
LSTM		*0.441*	*0.214*	*0.241*
Att-LSTM		*0.447*	*0.221*	*0.249*
Bert		*0.419*	*0.218*	*0.242*
Qwen 2.5(0.5b)		*0.333*	*0.160*	*0.178*
Qwen 2.5(1.5b)		*0.314*	*0.149*	*0.165*
DMQR		**0.455**	**0.228**	**0.256**
v-DMQR	**DIS**	**0.461**	**0.232**	**0.260**
	GEN	**0.460**	**0.233**	**0.261**
av-DMQR	**DIS**	**0.452**	**0.224**	**0.250**
	GEN	**0.453**	**0.224**	**0.251**

Second, our approach DMQR outperforms Att-LSTM by 0.8% on Recall, 0.7% on MAP and 0.7% on MRR, which offer the evidence for the effectiveness of knowledge mapping and medical knowledge to some degree.

Third, LSTM outperforms both the traditional machine learning approaches SVM and LM, showing the great advantages of the deep learning approach for sequence-related tasks.

Fourth, our approach DMQR outperforms large language models include Bert, Qwen 2.5(0.5b) and Qwen 2.5(1.5b), demonstrating the effectiveness of our knowledge mapping mechanism.

Finally, all metrics of both v-DMQR's discriminator and generator are about 0.5% and 0.6% higher than that in the DMQR, showing the effectiveness of the learning strategy. However, the performance of av-DMQR is not good as v-DMQR and DMQR. The primary reason is that we regard all questions answered by a physician as the documents of this physician. Specifically, the pseudo ground-truth probability of av-DMQR is computed based on this file rather than using the number of physicians whose names or email addresses are in the document, which could be inaccurate and contain a lot of noise. Another reason may be the result from the Eq. 9, in which we set n of s_n to 1. This means the pseudo ground-truth probability is the probability of a physician u having expertise on a word w. However, this physician-word probability could be more inaccurate considering the physician document is inaccurate.

6.2 The Effect of the Percentage of Medical Knowledge (RQ2)

To verify what impacts does the data have on our model DMQR, we carry out analytical experiments to compare the performance of DMQR with LSTM and Att-LSTM on two different datasets. These two datasets are divided from the Test dataset, one called **Empty**, does not contain any medical terminologies, while the other called **Non-Empty** has at least one medical terminology for each question. The divided datasets are showed as Table 4.

Table 4. The two divided datasets. # denotes the number of questions.

Dataset	Empty	Non-Empty	Test
#	10576	20180	30756

Furthermore, Table 5 shows the performance comparison among LSTM, Att-LSTM and our approach DMQR. For the Empty dataset, the MT extractor can't recognize any MT from the question, so the medical knowledge is not useful. We can see that our approach DMQR outperforms LSTM by 0.7% on Recall, 0.5% on MAP and 0.4% on MRR. These performance improvements might result from concatenating the original question representation twice when there is no medical terminology in question. However, the performance of this approach is keeping at least on the same level as LSTM. This indicates that the DMQR shows good robustness when the data have knowledge sparsity problems. Additionally, we can also see that the Att-LSTM shows better performances than DMQR on both MAP and MRR, 0.4% and 0.7% respectively. This phenomenon makes sense since the greatest strength of our DMQR approach is building the knowledge mapping between questions and physicians, we can not build this mapping mechanism without knowledge.

In the Non-Empty dataset, all of the questions have at least one medical terminology. We find that our method DMQR outperforms LSTM by 1.8% on Recall, 1.9% on MAP and even 2.1% on MRR. These improvements are larger than the improvements between DMQR and LSTM shown in Table 3. Compared with the phenomenon shown in the Empty dataset, DMQR shows better performances than Att-LSTM, 0.8% in terms of Recall, 1.3% on MAP and 1.0% on MRR. The improvement of the Recall metric is kept on the same level, as shown in Table 3, however, improvements of both the MAP and MRR are relatively higher than those in Table 3. This indicates that our DMQR approach can achieve better performances when the input data have abundant medical knowledge.

Table 5. Performance comparison between LSTM, Att-LSTM and DMQR on two datasets.

lMethods	Empty			Non-Empty		
	Recall	MAP	MRR	Recall	MAP	MRR
LSTM	0.422	0.189	0.214	0.450	0.227	0.255
Att-LSTM	0.428	**0.198**	**0.225**	0.456	0.233	0.262
DMQR	**0.429**	0.194	0.218	**0.468**	**0.246**	**0.276**

In conclusion, DMQR has good robustness when the data is difficult to model, and does not perform worse than most of the baselines. From another viewpoint, it shows great strength when the data contains abundant medical knowledge.

6.3 The Effect of Knowledge Mapping Mechanism (RQ3)

To examine the effects of attention and our knowledge mapping mechanism, we take the LSTM as a benchmark, and compare the performance improvements of Att-LSTM and DMQR with respect to LSTM. The attention improvements are generated by computing the performance difference between Att-LSTM and LSTM. And the knowledge improvements are generated by calculating the performance difference between DMQR and LSTM. For the convenience of comparison, we gather the corresponding results from Tables 3 and 5, shown in Table 6. We do not employ the performance results on the Empty dataset in Table 5, since the knowledge mapping mechanism is not working in this dataset.

In the Non-Empty dataset, the improvement of knowledge mapping is more observable than the improvements in attention mechanism on all three metrics, with the absolute improvement is 1.2% on Recall, 1.3% on MAP and 1.4%.

In the Test dataset, the improvements in knowledge mapping are also considerable compared with attention. However, the increments are slower than those in the Non-Empty dataset, this is because the Test dataset includes two subsets, Empty and Non-Empty. Just like the phenomenon illustrated in Table 5, the performance of DMQR is worse than the performances of Att-LSTM on the Empty dataset, which drags down the performance of DMQR on Test dataset.

Furthermore, the knowledge mapping mechanism can provide evidence that the matching physician has the expertise to advise about the disease. Thus, our

Table 6. The improvements comparison between attention and knowledge mapping mechanism. The benchmark of comparison is the performance of LSTM.

Performance Improvements	Non-Empty			Test		
	Recall	MAP	MRR	Recall	MAP	MRR
Attention	0.6%	0.6%	0.7%	0.6%	0.7%	0.8%
Knowledge Mapping	**1.8%**	**1.9%**	**2.1%**	**1.4%**	**1.4%**	**1.5%**

knowledge mapping mechanism is more suitable for the healthcare community, and it is more helpful than the attention mechanism in our dataset.

6.4 Case Studies

To analyze the effectiveness of the knowledge mapping mechanism, we select four representative routing examples in this section. Two examples of the situation that our model performs well, while the other two examples for the situation that our model can not handle. Examples are showed in Table 7. and each physician is represented as a ID number. in this table. For simplicity, we just show the top 10 physicians from the routing list.

As is showed in this table, the four examples are divided into two groups. One is the Group 1 in which our model performs very well, the other is the Group 2 containing the examples which our model can not handle. For the first example in Group 1, we can see that the MT extractor recognizes three medical terminologies from the question sequence, 'blood sugar', 'diabetes' and 'insulin'. There are no other potential medical terminologies that can convey crucial information about the disease in this question. Based on these three medical terminologies, we can guess that this patient is seeking medical suggestion about Diabetes, and physician No.76, a Physician specializing in Diabetes and Endocrinology has answered this question. We see that it is truly presented and its position of it in the routing list is the top one position. Furthermore, we can also find that the working area or specialties of the other 9 routed physicians are all about Diabetes or Endocrinology. Even though these physicians do not answer this question in reality, our model still routes them to this question. So does the second example in Group 1. From these two cases, we can conclude that our model performs very well when all the medical terminologies are recognized. Additionally, these cases also prove that our model can route the potential suitable physician to be the answerer of questions, not just the physician that has answered this question before.

However, there are also bad cases that our model cannot handle, such as the examples shown in Group 2. For the first example, the MT extractor does not recognize any medical terminologies from the question. So our model can not build the knowledge mapping between the questions and corresponding physicians. The reasons that our model can not handle this case are two-fold. First, there is a matching problem between the patient's description and specialized

Table 7. Examples of routing lists. ** means the corresponding word or phrase is recognized as MT. ✓ denotes the right physician. Each physician is represented as a ID number, and () means the physician's speciality or working area.

	Question	MTs	Ground Truths	Routing List
Group 1	Is it necessary to test a child's blood sugar if he has juvenile diabetes and is on insulin?	3	76(Endocrinology, Diabetes)	76(✓); 182(Pediatric,Endocrinology); 0(Pediatric,Thyroidea); 339(Pediatric,Diabetes); 32(Endocrinology,Nutrition); 68(Pediatric,Hepatitis); 302(Pediatric,Puberty); 155(Endocrine,Diabetes); 13(Pediatric,Vaccine); 7(Urology)
	What time of day is best to take ovulation meds like Clomiphene citrate?	2	80(Fertility Medicine); 237(Gynecology and Obstetrics)	237(✓); 80(✓); 185(Gynecology); 220(Gynecology and Obstetrics); 315(Gynecology); 346(Infertility); 475(Gynecology, Pregnancy); 57(Gynecology and Obstetrics); 396(Fertility,Contraception); 206(Infertility)
Group 2	My left leg hurts when I put pressure on it, what should I do?	0	65(Orthopedic, Gonitis)	349(Geriatric,Aortic Aneurysm); 401(Sports Medicine); 75(Podiatry); 49(podiatry,Diabetic Foot); 50(Radiology,CT); 239(Angioplasty); 16(Podiatry,Wart); 416(Radiology); 253(Orthopedic,Gonitis); 11(Orthopedic)
	At what age should I get eye laser surgery?	2	3(Women's Health,Diabetes)	60(Ophthalmology,Cataract); 73(Ophthalmology); 110(Ophthalmology,Optometry); 84(Ophthalmology); 452(Ophthalmology,Keratoplasty); 278(Cataract); 214(Glaucoma,Cataract); 192(Facial Plastic Surgery); 6(Ophthalmology); 314(Ophthalmology,Glaucoma)

medical knowledge, like 'leg pain' and 'Gonitis' in this example. Second, our knowledge base is imperfection, and there are tremendous medical terminologies that our KB does not contain. Additionally, considering the example in Group 2, there are two medical terminologies contained in this question, 'eye laser' and 'surgery'. However, the ground truth physician No.3 is a specialist of Women's Health and Diabetes area. So there are possibilities that, physicians whose primary working area is quite irrelevant to this disease also possess the knowledge to offer advices for the patients. Under this circumstance, our model can not achieve good performances.

7 Conclusion

In this study, we have introduced medical knowledge into QRHC, building a knowledge mapping between questions and physicians through knowledge triples. We have proposed a novel question routing model called Deep medical question routing(DMQR) in the healthcare community based on knowledge-graph. In this model, we have first designed an MT extractor to recognize and extract MT from the question. Then, we have employed a KB enquirer to retrieve corresponding triples by interacting with KB. Next, we have employed a knowledge graph embedding module to transform entities and relations into low-dimensional representations. Then, we have encoded the question sequence to question representation using the knowledge interpreter. Our knowledge mapping mechanism utilizes the knowledge-level expertise matching. We have conducted extensive experiments on a dataset collected from HealthTap, a community-based health service. We have confirmed that our DMQR approach outperforms state-of-the-art approaches in terms of Recall, MAP and MRR.

Our research can be applied in real-world community healthcare services, because our strategy focuses on knowledge-level question-physician matching, which generates tremendous medical facts. Additionally, we further enhance the robustness and efficiency of QpR by proposing a virtual adversarial medical question routing algorithm, v-DMQR, and an efficient version that uses anchor question-physician pairs, namely av-DMQR. DMQR can be extended from multiple aspects. For example, the strategy of recognizing and extracting MT from question can be more accurate and effective, and DMQR does not solve the matching problem between patient's descriptions and specialized knowledge. We will enhance our model in future work.

Acknowledgements. This work is supported by the National Key R&D Program of China (2022YFC3303004), the Natural Science Foundation of China (62372275, 61972234, 62102234, 622722 74, 62202271, 61902219, 62072279), the Key Scientific and Technological Innovation Program of Shandong Province (2019JZZY010129).

Disclosure of Interests. The authors have no competing interests to declare that are relevant to the content of this article.

References

1. Amancio, L., Dorneles, C.F., Dalip, D.H.: Recency and quality-based ranking question in CQAS: a stack overflow case study. Inf. Process. Manage. **58**(4), 102552 (2021)
2. Azzam, A., Tazi, N., Hossny, A.: A question routing technique using deep neural network for communities of question answering. In: DASFAA, pp. 35–49. Springer (2017)
3. Azzam, A., Tazi, N., Hossny, A.: Text-based question routing for question answering communities via deep learning. In: Proceedings of SAC, pp. 1674–1678. ACM (2017)

4. Balog, K., Azzopardi, L., De Rijke, M.: Formal models for expert finding in enterprise corpora. In: Proceedings of SIGIR, pp. 43–50 (2006)
5. Balog, K., Azzopardi, L., de Rijke, M.: A language modeling framework for expert finding. Inf. Process. Manage. **45**(1), 1–19 (2009)
6. Balog, K., et al.: Expertise retrieval. Found Trends INF RET **6**(2–3), 127–256 (2012)
7. Bhattacharya, P., Ghosh, K., Pal, A., Ghosh, S.: Legal case document similarity: you need both network and text. Inf. Process. Manage. **59**(6), 103069 (2022)
8. Bordes, A., Usunier, N., Garcia-Duran, A., Weston, J., Yakhnenko, O.: Translating embeddings for modeling multi-relational data. In: NIPS, pp. 2787–2795 (2013)
9. Borodin, A., Roberts, G.O., Rosenthal, J.S., Tsaparas, P.: Link analysis ranking: algorithms, theory, and experiments. ACM Trans. Internet Technol. **5**(1), 231–297 (2005)
10. Bouguessa, M., Dumoulin, B., Wang, S.: Identifying authoritative actors in question-answering forums: the case of yahoo! answers. In: Proceedings of ACM SIGKDD, pp. 866–874. ACM (2008)
11. Campbell, C.S., Maglio, P.P., Cozzi, A., Dom, B.: Expertise identification using email communications. In: Proceedings of CIKM, pp. 528–531. ACM (2003)
12. Chapelle, O., Metlzer, D., Zhang, Y., Grinspan, P.: Expected reciprocal rank for graded relevance. In: Proceedings of CIKM, pp. 621–630. Proceedings of CIKM, ACM (2009)
13. Cheng, X., Zhu, S., Su, S., Chen, G.: A multi-objective optimization approach for question routing in community question answering services. IEEE Trans. Knowl. Data Eng. **29**(9), 1779–1792 (2017)
14. Chowdhury, G.G.: Introduction to modern information retrieval. Facet publishing (2010)
15. Christopher, D.M., Prabhakar, R., Hinrich, S.: Introduction to information retrieval. Int. Inf. Retrieval **151**(177), 5 (2008)
16. Craswell, N.: Mean reciprocal rank. In: Encyclopedia of Database Systems, pp. 1703–1703. Springer (2009)
17. Craswell, N., Hawking, D., Vercoustre, A.M., Wilkins, P.: P@ noptic expert: searching for experts not just for documents. In: Ausweb Poster Proceedings, Queensland, Australia. vol. 15, p. 17 (2001)
18. Dehghan, M., Rahmani, H.A., Abin, A.A., Vu, V.V.: Mining shape of expertise: a novel approach based on convolutional neural network. Inf. Process. Manage. **57**(4), 102239 (2020)
19. Dom, B., Eiron, I., Cozzi, A., Zhang, Y.: Graph-based ranking algorithms for e-mail expertise analysis. In: Proceedings of ACM SIGMOD, pp. 42–48. ACM (2003)
20. Fu, Y., Xiang, R., Liu, Y., Zhang, M., Ma, S.: A CDD-based formal model for expert finding. In: Proceedings of CIKM, pp. 881–884. ACM (2007)
21. Guo, J., Xu, S., Bao, S., Yu, Y.: Tapping on the potential of q&a community by recommending answer providers. In: Proceedings of CIKM, pp. 921–930. ACM (2008)
22. Haveliwala, T.H.: Topic-sensitive pagerank. In: Proceedings of WWW, pp. 517–526. ACM (2002)
23. Hearst, M.A., Dumais, S.T., Osuna, E., Platt, J., Scholkopf, B.: Support vector machines. IEEE Intell. Syst. their appl. **13**(4), 18–28 (1998)
24. Hochreiter, S., Schmidhuber, J.: Long short-term memory. Neural Comput. **9**(8), 1735–1780 (1997)
25. Horowitz, D., Kamvar, S.D.: The anatomy of a large-scale social search engine. In: Proceedings of WWW, pp. 431–440. ACM (2010)

26. Hui, B., et al.: Qwen2.5-coder technical report. ArXiv **abs/2409.12186** (2024). https://api.semanticscholar.org/CorpusID:272707390
27. Jurczyk, P., Agichtein, E.: Discovering authorities in question answer communities by using link analysis. In: Proceedings of CIKM, pp. 919–922. ACM (2007)
28. Kenton, J.D.M.W.C., Toutanova, L.K.: Bert: pre-training of deep bidirectional transformers for language understanding. In: Proceedings of NAACL-HLT. vol. 1. Minneapolis, Minnesota (2019)
29. Li, B., King, I.: Routing questions to appropriate answerers in community question answering services. In: Proceedings of CIKM, pp. 1585–1588. ACM (2010)
30. Li, B., King, I., Lyu, M.R.: Question routing in community question answering: putting category in its place. In: Proceedings of CIKM, pp. 2041–2044. ACM (2011)
31. Liang, S., de Rijke, M.: Formal language models for finding groups of experts. Inf. Process. Manage. **52**(4), 529–549 (2016)
32. Liu, D.R., Chen, Y.H., Kao, W.C., Wang, H.W.: Integrating expert profile, reputation and link analysis for expert finding in question-answering websites. Inf. Process. Manage. **49**(1), 312–329 (2013)
33. Liu, X., Bollen, J., Nelson, M.L., Van de Sompel, H.: Co-authorship networks in the digital library research community. Inf. Process. Manage. **41**(6), 1462–1480 (2005)
34. Liu, X., Croft, W.B., Koll, M.: Finding experts in community-based question-answering services. In: Proceedings of CIKM, pp. 315–316. ACM (2005)
35. Liu, Z., Li, K., Qu, D.: Knowledge graph based question routing for community question answering. In: ICAIP, pp. 721–730. Springer (2017)
36. Macina, J., Srba, I., Williams, J.J., Bielikova, M.: Educational question routing in online student communities. In: RecSys '17, pp. 47–55. ACM (2017)
37. Nasrabadi, N.M.: Pattern recognition and machine learning. J. Electron. Imaging **16**(4), 049901 (2007)
38. Neshati, M., Fallahnejad, Z., Beigy, H.: On dynamicity of expert finding in community question answering. Inf. Process. Manage. **53**(5), 1026–1042 (2017)
39. Nie, L., Davison, B.D., Wu, B.: From whence does your authority come? utilizing community relevance in ranking. In: Proceedings of AAAI. vol. 7, pp. 1421–1426 (2007)
40. Nie, L., Zhang, L., Yan, Y., Chang, X., Liu, M., Shaoling, L.: Multiview physician-specific attributes fusion for health seeking. IEEE Trans. cybern. **47**(11), 3680–3691 (2017)
41. Qiu, Y., Ding, S., Tian, D., Zhang, C., Zhou, D.: Predicting the quality of answers with less bias in online health question answering communities. Inf. Process. Manage. **59**(6), 103112 (2022)
42. Qu, M., Qiu, G., He, X., Zhang, C., Wu, H., Bu, J., Chen, C.: Probabilistic question recommendation for question answering communities. In: Proceedings of WWW, pp. 1229–1230. ACM (2009)
43. Riahi, F., Zolaktaf, Z., Shafiei, M., Milios, E.: Finding expert users in community question answering. In: Proceedings of WWW, pp. 791–798. ACM (2012)
44. Rocktäschel, T., Grefenstette, E., Hermann, K.M., Kočiský, T., Blunsom, P.: Reasoning about entailment with neural attention. arXiv preprint arXiv:1509.06664 (2015)
45. Salakhutdinov, R., Hinton, G.: Semantic hashing. Int. J. Approximate Reasoning **50**(7), 969–978 (2009)
46. Sun, J., Vishnu, A., Chakrabarti, A., Siegel, C., Parthasarathy, S.: Coldroute: effective routing of cold questions in stack exchange sites. Data Min. Knowl. Disc. **32**(5), 1339–1367 (2018)

47. Szegedy, C., et al.: Intriguing properties of neural networks. ICLR. 2014. arXiv preprint arXiv:1312.6199 **1** (2014)
48. Ting, K.M.: Precision and recall. In: Encyclopedia of machine learning, pp. 781–781. Springer (2011)
49. Wang, H.C., Yang, C.T., Yen, Y.H.: Answer selection and expert finding in community question answering services: a question answering promoter. Program **51**(1), 17–34 (2017)
50. Weng, J., Lim, E.P., Jiang, J., He, Q.: Twitterrank: finding topic-sensitive influential twitterers. In: Proceedings of WSDM, pp. 261–270. ACM (2010)
51. Wu, D., Fan, S., Yuan, F.: Research on pathways of expert finding on academic social networking sites. Inf. Process. Manage. **58**(2), 102475 (2021)
52. Wu, Y., Zhao, S., Guo, R.: A novel community answer matching approach based on phrase fusion heterogeneous information network. Inf. Process. Manage. **58**(1), 102408 (2021)
53. Yan, Z., Zhou, J.: Optimal answerer ranking for new questions in community question answering. Inf. Process. Manage. **51**(1), 163–178 (2015)
54. Zhang, J., Ackerman, M.S., Adamic, L.: Expertise networks in online communities: structure and algorithms. In: Proceedings of WWW, pp. 221–230. ACM (2007)
55. Zhou, G., Lai, S., Liu, K., Zhao, J.: Topic-sensitive probabilistic model for expert finding in question answer communities. In: Proceedings of CIKM, pp. 1662–1666. ACM (2012)
56. Zhou, Y., Cong, G., Cui, B., Jensen, C.S., Yao, J.: Routing questions to the right users in online communities. In: ICDE, pp. 700–711. IEEE (2009)
57. Zhu, M.: Recall, precision and average precision. Depart. Stat. Actuarial Sci. Univ. Waterloo, Waterloo **2**, 30 (2004)

A Comparative Study of Specialized LLMs as Dense Retrievers

Hengran Zhang[1,2,3(✉)], Keping Bi[1,2,3], and Jiafeng Guo[1,2,3]

[1] Key Laboratory of Network Data Science and Technology, Institute of Computing Technology, Chinese Academy of Sciences, Beijing, China
{zhanghengran22z,bikeping,guojiafeng}@ict.ac.cn
[2] State Key Laboratory of AI Safety, Beijing, China
[3] University of Chinese Academy of Sciences, Beijing, China

Abstract. While large language models (LLMs) are increasingly deployed as dense retrievers, the impact of their domain-specific specialization on retrieval effectiveness remains underexplored. This investigation systematically examines how task-specific adaptations in LLMs influence their retrieval capabilities—an essential step toward developing unified retrievers capable of handling text, code, images, and multimodal content. We conduct extensive experiments with eight Qwen2.5 7B LLMs, including base, instruction-tuned, code/math-specialized, long reasoning, and vision-language models across zero-shot retrieval settings and the supervised setting. For the zero-shot retrieval settings, we consider text retrieval from the BEIR benchmark and code retrieval from the CoIR benchmark. Further, to evaluate supervised performance, all LLMs are fine-tuned on the MS MARCO dataset. We find that mathematical specialization and the long reasoning capability cause consistent degradation in three settings, indicating conflicts between mathematical reasoning and semantic matching. The vision-language model and code-specialized LLMs demonstrate superior zero-shot performance compared to other LLMs, even surpassing BM25 on the code retrieval task, and maintain comparable performance to base LLMs in supervised settings. These findings suggest promising directions for the unified retrieval task leveraging cross-domain and cross-modal fusion.

Keywords: Dense Retrieval · Large Language Models · Specialized LLMs

1 Introduction

First-stage retrieval plays a crucial role in information access, serving as the foundation for downstream processes such as re-ranking or augmenting generation. Its primary goal is to retrieve as many relevant documents as possible from a large-scale corpus, which may contain millions or even billions of entries. Traditionally, term-based retrieval methods like BM25 [26] have faced challenges such as vocabulary mismatch due to their reliance on lexical matching between

Z. Li et al. (Eds.): CCIR 2025, LNCS 16369, pp. 49–61, 2026.
https://doi.org/10.1007/978-981-95-5637-3_4

query and document terms. Over time, retrieval techniques have evolved from these classical term-based approaches to neural retrievers like DRMM [12]. More recently, retrievers based on pre-trained language models (PLMs) have become prevalent. Known as dense retrieval, PLM-based retrieval typically employs a dual encoder mechanism that encodes queries and documents into embeddings, assessing their relevance using functions like dot product or cosine similarity [17].

The emergence of large language models (LLMs) such as Qwen series [36], GPT series [1], and DeepSeek [20] has shown compelling language understanding and generation capabilities. This makes it appealing to researchers to study how to leverage them for dense retrieval. Recent studies indicate that LLMs also show strong potential in dense retrieval tasks. For instance, Llama fine-tuned with MS MARCO significantly outperforms BERT-based retrievers [22].

There are various types of LLMs tuned specifically for different tasks or domains, such as those specialized for code generation [15], mathematical reasoning [37], text generation [36], multi-modal tasks [3], and so on. Although LLMs have been shown to be powerful as dense retrievers, their specialized capabilities could have a different impact on their retrieval performance if they are used as dense retrievers. For example, do the coding or mathematical reasoning capability negatively impact LLMs' text retrieval potential? Will more competent LLMs, such as long-reasoning and multi-modal models, be better backbones as denser retrievers? Studies on these questions will provide insights into understanding the impact of LLMs' specialty on their capabilities as dense retrievers. This is also beneficial for developing a unified retriever that can handle the retrieval of text, code, image, etc. Therefore, in this paper, we present a comprehensive investigation into the relationship between LLMs' specialty and their retrieval performance.

To ensure methodological rigor and comparative fairness in our experiments, we conducted a comprehensive evaluation of domain-specialized language models using eight Qwen2.5 variants as retrieval backbones, i.e., Qwen-2.5-7B, Qwen-2.5-7B-Instruct, Qwen2.5-7B-Coder, Qwen2.5-7B-Coder-Instruct, Qwen2.5-7B-Math, Qwen2.5-7B-Math-Instruct, Qwen2.5-7B-VL-Instruct and Deepseek-R1-distill-Qwen-7B. We employ three settings: 1. zero-shot text retrieval setting (low-resource datasets from the BEIR benchmark [29]); 2. zero-shot code retrieval setting (CoIR benchmark [19]); 3. supervised training setting (MS MARCO and TREC DL19/20). Our systematic investigation yielded the following principal findings through rigorous experimental analysis: 1. **zero-shot text retrieval setting**: Code-specialized LLMs and the vision-language model demonstrated superior performance compared to other LLMs. This highlights the advantage of multimodal understanding and code-centric pretraining in text retrieval scenarios. 2. **zero-shot code retrieval setting**: Vision-language models and code-specialized LLMs demonstrate superior zero-shot performance compared to other LLMs, even surpassing BM25. 3. **supervised training setting**: After supervised training, the vision-language model and code-specialized LLMs maintain comparable performance to base models. Other specialized LLMs exhibited significant degradation in retrieval tasks.

In Summary: The long-reasoning LLM and mathematics-specialized LLMs consistently underperformed across all three settings. This implies that models optimized for logical reasoning tasks may lack effectiveness in global semantic retrieval, which prioritizes contextual understanding over stepwise deduction. Moreover, the robust performance of the vision-language model and code-specialized LLMs suggests promising directions for the unified retrieval task leveraging cross-domain and cross-modal fusion.

2 Related Work

Passage Retrieval. Passage retrieval focuses on finding relevant information from extensive passage repositories based on the search queries using retrieval models. Conventional retrieval approaches such as TF-IDF and the probabilistic BM25 model [26] primarily rely on lexical term matching and inverse document frequency calculations for relevance measurement. While these algorithms demonstrate notable efficiency in retrieval operations, they are fundamentally constrained by lexical mismatch issues [11]. Dense Retrieval (DR) becomes another popular retrieval model, encoding queries and documents into dense vector representations and measuring relevance through similarity computations. This section will briefly introduce different dense retrieval models: pre-trained language models-based dense retriever (PLM-based DR) and large language models-based dense retriever (LLM-based DR).

2.1 PLM-Based DR

To further enhance dense retrieval methods based on pre-trained language models, advancements have been made in two key areas: 1. customized pre-training for dense retrieval [6,21,33]: For example, RetroMAE [33] employed masked auto-encoder (MAE) frameworks tailored for IR. These methods introduce a shallow decoder to reconstruct the original input from masked tokens and sentence embeddings, enhancing the modelâĂŹs ability to generate meaningful representations for retrieval purposes. Other works, such as those by [6], propose paragraph-level pre-training tasks like the Inverse Cloze Task (ICT) to better capture contextual relationships between queries and documents. 2. hard negative mining: For example, RocketQA [25] enhances retrieval performance through cross-batch negatives and denoised hard negatives.

2.2 LLM-Based DR

The emergence of Large Language Models (LLMs) like Qwen [2], and GPT-4 [1] has demonstrated exceptional performance in various domains, particularly in natural language generation. Recent studies [22,27] have explored incorporating decoder-only LLM architectures into dense retrieval systems, encoding queries and documents into embeddings for similarity comparison. For instance,

RepLLaMA [22] replaces PLMs with LLMs for encoding and shows that even with simple fine-tuning strategies, LLM-based retrievers can surpass PLM-based retrievers that employ more complex training methods. LLM2VEC [4] modifies the decoder-only architecture to include bidirectional attention mechanisms, further improving retrieval effectiveness. Llama2Vec [18] introduces pre-training tasks such as Embedding-based Auto-Encoding and Embedding-based Auto-Regression to better adapt LLMs for dense retrieval applications. Echo [28] tackles architectural limitations by repeating inputs in the context and extracting embeddings from subsequent occurrences. LLM-QL [38] proposed query likelihood modeling training before conservative learning to enhance retrieval performance.

3 LLM-Based Retrieval

Dense Retrieval (DR) is a retrieval framework that learns dense vector representations of queries and passages through dual-tower encoders. Given a query q and a passage p, the model computes their embeddings as:

$$\mathbf{h}_q = E_Q(q) \in \mathbb{R}^d, \quad \mathbf{h}_p = E_P(p) \in \mathbb{R}^d \tag{1}$$

where $E_Q(\cdot)$ and $E_P(\cdot)$ denote the query and passage encoders, respectively, and d is the embedding dimension.

Training Strategy: Contrastive Learning. The model is trained to maximize the similarity between queries and relevant passages while minimizing similarity with non-relevant ones. For each query-positive passage pair (q, p^+), we construct negative examples $\{p_i^-\}_{i=1}^N$ containing both hard negatives and in-batch negatives. The training is then optimized according to contrastive learning:

$$\mathcal{L} = -\log \frac{e^{s(q,p^+)}}{e^{s(q,p^+)} + \sum_{i=1}^N e^{s(q,p_i^-)}} \tag{2}$$

where $s(q,p) =< \mathbf{h}_q, \mathbf{h}_p >$ is the similarity score between the query and document measured by dot product or cosine similarity.

4 Experimental Setup

4.1 LLMs

Qwen2.5. Qwen2.5 [36] maintains the Transformer-based decoder architecture [30] of Qwen2 [35]. Compared to Qwen2, Qwen2.5 has a larger and higher-quality pre-training dataset, expanding from 7 trillion tokens to 18 trillion tokens. The pre-training data spans various domains, including e-commerce, social media, and entertainment, as well as mathematical data from Qwen2.5 Math [37] and coding data from Qwen2.5 Coder [15]. The Qwen2.5-Instruct model is derived from Qwen2.5 through post-training involving supervised fine-tuning and reinforcement learning.

Qwen2.5 Math. Qwen2.5 Math [37] is obtained by further pre-training the Qwen2.5 model on high-quality mathematical data, specifically the Qwen Math Corpus v2, which contains over 1 trillion tokens. After completing this pre-training, Qwen2.5-Math-Instruct is fine-tuned using Chain-of-Thought (CoT) and Tool-Integrated Reasoning (TIR) methods on the Qwen2.5 Math base model.

Qwen2.5 Coder. Qwen2.5 Coder [15] is trained on a large-scale, coding-specific pre-training dataset comprising over 5.5 trillion tokens, sourced from a wide range of public code repositories such as GitHub and extensive web-crawled data containing code-related texts. The dataset includes five types: Source Code Data, Text-Code Grounding Data, Synthetic Data, Math Data, and Text Data. Balancing code, math, and text data is crucial for building a foundational model; it was found that a 7:2:1 ratio outperformed other configurations. Qwen2.5-Code-Instruct is fine-tuned using Supervised Fine-Tuning (SFT) and Direct Preference Optimization (DPO) on the Qwen2.5 Coder base model.

DeepSeek-R1-Distill-Qwen. DeepSeek-R1-Distill-Qwen [10], obtained by directly distilling DeepSeek-R1 into the Qwen2.5 [36] model, outperforms the approach of applying reinforcement learning to Qwen2.5.

Qwen2.5 VL. Qwen2.5-VL [3] introduces significant vision-language advancements over its predecessor, including enhanced omnidocument parsing for multilingual, multi-scene texts and specialized formats (tables, formulas, etc.), improved object grounding accuracy with spatial reasoning in JSON/coordinate formats, and ultra-long video understanding via dynamic resolution/frame-rate training for temporal event extraction. Specifically, Qwen2.5-VL contains a large language model that is initialized with pre-trained weights from the Qwen2.5 LLM, a vision encoder that is a redesigned Vision Transformer (ViT) architecture, and a two-layer multi-layer perceptron(MLP) that projects vision features into a dimension that aligns with the text embeddings used in the LLM.

4.2 Datasets

CoIR Benchamrk. To verify the domain capability on retrieval performance, we evaluate code retrieval datasets on the CoIR benchmark [19]: 1) Text-to-Code Retrieval (T2C): a. APPS [13], which is a diverse collection of problems from platforms; b. CosQA [14], which contains labeled pairs of textual queries and Python functions; c. Synthetic-Text2Sql, which is the largest and most diverse synthetic dataset. 2) Code-to-Text Retrieval (C2C): a. CodeTrans [34], which contains code written within the same programming language, i.e., CodeTrans-Contest, and different programming languages, i.e., CodeTrans-DL; b. CodeSearchNet-CCR, which is the modified dataset from the original CodeSearchNet. 3) Code-to-Text Retrieval (C2T): a. CodeSearchNet [16], which consists of numerous code functions accompanied by code comments. 3) Hybrid

Code Retrieval (Hybrid): a. Stackoverflow-QA[1], which is derived from the original StackOverflow dataset by pairing questions with their highest upvoted answers; b. Codefeedback [39], which is a synthesized code instruction dataset generated by LLMs, contains Codefeedback-MT and CodeFeedBack-ST.

BEIR Benchmark. We consider low-resource datasets from the BEIR [29], so we employ six datasets, consisting of question-answering task: FiQA [23] and Quora; citation-prediction task: SCIDOCS [7]; bio-medical IR task: TREC-COVID [31] and NFcorpus [5]; argument retrieval task: ArguAna [32].

MS MARCO. In our experiments, we utilize the MS MARCO passage retrieval dataset [24] for both training and evaluation purposes. We train different Qwen models on the MS MARCO training set, which includes about 500K queries. For evaluation, we employ three datasets: MS MARCO-dev, TREC-DL19 and TREC DL20 [8]. The MS MARCO-dev set consists of 6,980 queries, each associated with an average of 1.1 relevant passages.

4.3 Zero-Shot Details

For zero-shot retrieval performance evaluation, the design of prompts significantly impacts model performance. We adopt the prompts from previous work [40], which have been proven effective in text retrieval tasks. The specific prompts are formulated as follows: 1. **Prompt for document:** “Passage: “[text]”. Use one word to represent the passage in a retrieval task. Make sure your word is in lowercase. <A> The word is: “”. 2. **Prompt for query:** Prompt for query representation: “Query: “[text]”. Use one word to represent the query in a retrieval task. Make sure your word is in lowercase. <A> The word is: “”. “<A>” denotes the model-specific assistant special token. The hidden state of the last token “ as the query or document embedding. To ensure fair comparison across all zero-shot retrieval tasks, identical prompts are consistently used for all LLMs.

4.4 Training Details

All Qwen models are trained with Deepseed, which is an efficient deep-learning optimization library, and Zero Redundancy Optimizer-3 (ZeRO-3), which is a family of memory optimization technologies for large-scale distributed deep learning. For hard negative mining, we adopt the methodology established in RepLLaMA [22], implementing a hybrid approach combining BM25 lexical retrieval with CoCondenser [9] dense retrieval. This dual-channel selection mechanism ensures comprehensive coverage of challenging negative samples from both sparse and dense representation spaces. Following [22], the training protocol employs a single epoch with a global batch size of 32 (achieved through 4 gradient accumulation steps on 8 NVIDIA A800 GPUs with 80GB memory). The optimization process utilizes the AdamW optimizer with an initial learning rate of 1e-4, maintaining hardware utilization efficiency through ZeRO-3 parallelism.

[1] https://www.kaggle.com/datasets/stackoverflow/stacksample/data.

Table 1. Zero-shot NDCG@10 retrieval performance on text retrieval datasets. "Base", "Instruct", "Coder", "Coder-I", "Math", "Math-I", "Distill", and "VL-I" are "Qwen2.5-7B", "Qwen2.5-7B-Instruct", "Qwen2.5-coder-7B", "Qwen2.5-coder-7B-Instruct", "Qwen2.5-math-7B", "Qwen2.5-math-7B-Instruct", "Deepseek-R1-Distill-Qwen-7B", and "Qwen2.5-VL-7B-Instruct", respectively. **Bold** means the best performance.

Dataset	BM25	Base	Instruct	Coder	Coder-I	Math	Math-I	Distill	VL-I
FiQA	0.2361	0.1239	0.1819	0.2192	0.2482	0.0731	0.1192	0.1237	**0.2531**
SCIDOCS	0.1490	0.1356	0.1365	0.1527	**0.1784**	0.1302	0.0853	0.0976	0.1601
TREC-COVID	0.5947	0.5622	0.5060	0.5566	0.5643	0.3869	0.4364	0.4181	**0.6094**
NFcorpus	**0.3218**	0.2045	0.2237	0.1928	0.2793	0.1148	0.1673	0.1200	0.2447
Quora	0.7886	0.7202	0.6936	**0.8024**	0.7952	0.5211	0.6834	0.7199	0.7799
ArguAna	**0.3970**	0.3229	0.1882	0.3304	0.2772	0.2926	0.1696	0.2195	0.2507
Avg	**0.4145**	0.3449	0.3217	0.3757	0.3904	0.2531	0.2769	0.2831	0.3830

We use the parameter-efficient tuning method, i.e., LoRA with the LoRA rank of 32. Moreover, we can extract the final-layer hidden state representation of the end-of-sequence (EOS) special token in LLMs as the dense representation for the query or document. The prompts for the query and document are "Query:" and "Passage:", respectively.

5 Experiment Results

5.1 Zero-Shot Text Retrieval Results

We evaluate the zero-shot NDCG@10 retrieval performance of various specialized LLMs against the BM25 baseline across six datasets from the BEIR benchmark, as shown in Table 1. Key observations are summarized as follows:

1) **Domain-specialized LLMs outperform general-purpose LLMs**. Models with code-specific pertaining and multimodal tuning demonstrate superior retrieval capabilities. The coder-oriented variants (Coder: 0.3757, Coder-I: 0.3904) and vision-language model (VL-I: 0.3830) achieve average performance exceeding the base model (0.3449), with Qwen2.5-VL-7B-Instruct showing best performance on biomedical (trec-covid: 0.6094) and financial (FiQA: 0.2531) queries. This suggests that specific domain adaptation for LLMs can enhance zero-shot retrieval effectiveness.
2) **Instruction tuning has variable impacts**. The effect of instruction tuning varies significantly across model specializations. Instruction tuning of base models demonstrates a pronounced adverse impact on retrieval task performance. However, domain-adapted LLMs necessitate subsequent instruction tuning to attain improved comprehension of retrieval tasks. For example, while instruction tuning is beneficial for coder models (+3.9% CoderâĘŠCoder-Instruct and 9.4% MathâĘŠMath-Instruct), it degrades performance in base models (-6.7% BaseâĘŠInstruct).

Table 2. Zero-shot NDCG@10 retrieval performance on code retrieval datasets. **Bold**, "Base", "Instruct", "Coder", "Coder-I", "Math", "Math-I", "Distill", and "VL-I" are defined in Table 1. "S-T", "CF-", "CT-" "CS", "CT-C" and "SK-" are the "Synthetic-Text2Sql", "CodeFeedBack-", "CodeTrans-", "CodeSearchNet", "CodeTrans-Contest" and "Stackoverflow-", respectively.

Task	Dataset	BM25	Base	Instruct	Coder	Coder-I	Math	Math-I	Distill	VL-I
T2C	APPS	0.0095	0.0162	0.0774	0.0732	0.1611	0.0325	0.0773	0.0449	**0.1948**
	CosQA	0.1396	0.0759	0.2128	0.2193	0.2677	0.1213	0.1750	0.1646	**0.2519**
	S-T	0.1692	0.2880	0.0863	**0.5135**	0.4840	0.3380	0.2646	0.2268	0.2874
C2T	CS	0.2675	0.2632	0.0891	**0.3737**	0.3699	0.1584	0.2260	0.2619	0.2067
C2C	CT-C	0.5013	0.2320	0.2756	0.3163	0.3453	0.1753	0.3105	0.1456	**0.7813**
	CT-DL	0.0869	0.1599	0.1706	0.1602	0.1749	0.1007	0.1471	0.1883	**0.2942**
	CS-CCR	**0.3469**	0.2123	0.1520	0.2760	0.3005	0.1544	0.2001	0.1720	0.3360
Hybird	SK-QA	0.5680	0.4000	0.3069	0.4790	0.4926	0.2109	0.2798	0.2535	**0.6169**
	CF-MT	0.3473	0.0758	0.0701	0.1126	0.0938	0.0519	0.0698	0.0481	**0.5070**
	CF-ST	0.5432	0.2378	0.2962	0.4699	0.4468	0.2284	0.3096	0.2612	**0.5666**
Avg		0.2979	0.1961	0.1737	0.2994	0.3137	0.1572	0.2060	0.1767	**0.4043**

3) **Long reasoning reduces retrieval performance**. While test-time scaling demonstrates substantial advantages in question answering and related tasks, it has been observed to exhibit markedly diminished performance in retrieval scenarios. For example, the retrieval performance of the long reasoning LLM decreased by 17.9% compared to the base model in terms of NDCG@10. This discrepancy may stem from fundamental task objective misalignment: retrieval systems primarily require global semantic alignment, whereas question-answering and reasoning tasks demand granular comprehension of contextual details.
4) **Mathematical specialization hinders general retrieval**. Mathematical LLM demonstrates the weakest performance, underperforming even Deepseel-R1-Distill-Qwen-7B. This observation suggests that retrieval tasks may not necessitate sophisticated logical-mathematical reasoning capabilities.

In summary. Coding specialized pertaining and multimodal capability significantly impacts zero-shot retrieval effectiveness. Long reasoning and mathematical conflicts in global semantic matching result in worse retrieval performance. These findings suggest coding specialized pertaining and multimodal capabilities as promising directions for generalizable text retrieval tasks.

5.2 Zero-Shot Code Retrieval

Table 2 examines the zero-shot NDCG@10 performance of specialized LLMs for code retrieval on the CoIR benchmark. Key findings are summarized as follows:

1) **Multimodal pretraining achieves best code retrieval performance.** The vision-language model Qwen2.5-VL-7B-Instruct achieves the best code retrieval performance and outperforms BM25 by 48% in terms of average NDCG@10. This suggests that cross-modal training enhances code representation learning through improved structural understanding.
2) **Code-specialized LLMs achieve superior code retrieval performance.** Models pre-trained on code-centric objectives demonstrate significant advantages compared to the base LLM. The average performance of the instruction-tuned coder variant is improved by 66% compared to the base LLM. This highlights the critical role of code-aligned pretraining for semantic code matching.
3) **Instruction tuning amplifies code retrieval capabilities.** Instruction tuning consistently improves code retrieval performance across different domain-specific LLMs, e.g., coder, and math LLMs. This demonstrates the generalizability of instruction tuning for zero-shot code retrieval tasks.
4) **Mathematical pretraining shows worst code retrieval Performance.** Similar to text retrieval performance, the math-adaption LLM has the worst performance, which further indicates that limited cross-domain transfer between mathematical reasoning and semantic matching.
5) **Long reasoning compromises code retrieval performance.** The performance of the long reasoning LLM is decreased by 10.3% compared to the base LLM in terms of NDCG@10, suggesting reasoning techniques may disproportionately affect code retrieval, which is similar to the text retrieval task.

In summary. The vision-language model and code-specialized LLMs achieve superior zero-shot code retrieval performance compared to other LLMs, even compressing BM25. The experimental findings substantiate that cross-modal interactions and code structure comprehension exhibit alignment, thereby

Table 3. Different retrieval performance using different LLMs on MS MARCO and TREC DL 19/20. "$^-$" indicate significant decrements over Qwen2.5-7B, using a two-sided paired t-test ($p < 0.05$). **Bold** indicates the best performance.

LLM	DEV					DL19	DL20
	M@10	N@10	R@100	R@200	R@1000	N@10	N@10
Qwen2.5-7B	**0.423**	0.491	0.945	**0.973**	**0.995**	0.734	0.723
Qwen2.5-7B-instruct	**0.423**	**0.492**	**0.945**	**0.973**	0.994	**0.740**	0.729
Qwen2.5-coder-7B	0.419	0.489	0.944	0.970	0.995	0.733	**0.742**
Qwen2.5-coder-7B-instruct	0.418	0.488	0.944	0.969$^-$	0.995	0.733	0.734
Qwen2.5-math-7b	0.415$^-$	0.484$^-$	0.939$^-$	0.965$^-$	0.993$^-$	0.738	0.721
Qwen2.5-math-7b-instruct	0.413$^-$	0.480$^-$	0.934$^-$	0.964$^-$	0.992$^-$	0.727	0.715
Deepseek-R1-distill-Qwen-7B	0.413$^-$	0.481$^-$	0.935$^-$	0.966$^-$	0.992$^-$	0.737	0.703
Qwen2.5-VL-7B-instruct	0.418$^-$	0.488	0.943	0.969$^-$	0.994	0.727	0.739

enabling global semantic matching. Similar to zero-shot text retrieval, the long reasoning LLM and mathematical LLMs show worse retrieval performance, further indicating that reasoning and mathematical logic are not alignment with global semantic matching. The observed performance decline in the long-reasoning LLM likely stems from missing intermediate reasoning steps, though untested due to computational constraints, warranting further investigation.

5.3 Supervised Performance

Table 3 shows the supervised retrieval performance upon different LLMs. We can observe that:

Capability Specialization Impacts. Retrievers upon different specialized LLMs after contrastive learning reveal distinct retrieval performance. Coding-oriented variants and the vision-language model maintain comparable performance to the general base LLM on the DEV set on most metrics. Qwen2.5-coder-7B retriever achieves the best performance on TREC DL20 and has a similar performance on TREC DL19 with Qwen2.5-7B retriever. However, mathematical and reasoning specialization causes consistent degradation across all DEV metrics (e.g., -1.8% NDCG@10 for Qwen2.5-math-7b). Moreover, Qwen2.5-math-7B-instruct and Deepseek-R1-distill-Qwen-7B retrievers also achieve the worst performance on TRECL DL19 and TREC DL20, respectively. This suggests that mathematical abstraction may conflict with global semantic matching requirements in text retrieval tasks. The reasoning LLMs, i.e., Deepseek-R1-distill-Qwen-7B, which are effective in generation tasks such as question answering, have significantly reduced performance in retrieval tasks after supervised training. The possible reason is that retrieval tasks do not require complex reasoning but rely on the representation of global semantics.

6 Conclusion

We present a comprehensive investigation into the relationship between LLMs' specialty and their retrieval performance across supervised and zero-shot settings. We conduct extensive experiments using eight Qwen2.5-7B LLMs on zero-shot text/code settings and supervised settings. We observe three key findings: (1) Mathematical specialization and long reasoning LLMs cause consistent degradation in all three settings, indicating conflicts between mathematical reasoning and semantic matching; (2) Code-specialized and vision-language models demonstrate superior zero-shot performance compared to other LLMs and maintain comparable performance to base LLMs in supervised settings. The robust performance of the vision-language model and coding-specialized LLMs suggests promising directions for the unified retrieval task leveraging cross-domain and cross-modal fusion. The significant performance degradation of long-reasoning LLMs across three settings may potentially stem from the absence of the model to output its intermediate reasoning (thinking) process. However, due to the computational costs associated with generating extensive outputs from LLMs, this aspect was not tested in the current study and merits further investigation in future work.

Acknowledgment. This work was funded by the National Natural Science Foundation of China (NSFC) under Grants No. 62302486, the Innovation Project of ICT CAS under Grants No. E361140, the CAS Special Research Assistant Funding Project, the project under Grants No. JCKY2022130C039, the Strategic Priority Research Program of the CAS under Grants No. XDB0680102, and the NSFC Grant No. 62441229.

References

1. Achiam, J., Adler, S., Agarwal, S., et al.: Gpt-4 technical report. arXiv preprint arXiv:2303.08774 (2023)
2. Bai, J., et al.: Qwen technical report. arXiv preprint arXiv:2309.16609 (2023)
3. Bai, S., Chen, K., Liu, X., et al.: Qwen2. 5-vl technical report. arXiv preprint arXiv:2502.13923 (2025)
4. BehnamGhader, P., Adlakha, V., Mosbach, M., Bahdanau, D., Chapados, N., Reddy, S.: Llm2vec: large language models are secretly powerful text encoders. arXiv preprint arXiv:2404.05961 (2024)
5. Boteva, V., Gholipour, D., Sokolov, A., Riezler, S.: A full-text learning to rank dataset for medical information retrieval. In: Advances in Information Retrieval: 38th European Conference on IR Research, pp. 716–722. Springer (2016)
6. Chang, W.C., Yu, F.X., Chang, Y.W., Yang, Y., Kumar, S.: Pre-training tasks for embedding-based large-scale retrieval. arXiv preprint arXiv:2002.03932 (2020)
7. Cohan, A., Feldman, S., Beltagy, I., Downey, D., Weld, D.S.: Specter: document-level representation learning using citation-informed transformers. arXiv preprint arXiv:2004.07180 (2020)
8. Craswell, N., Mitra, B., Yilmaz, E., Campos, D., Voorhees, E.M.: Overview of the trec 2019 deep learning track. arXiv preprint arXiv:2003.07820 (2020)
9. Gao, L., Callan, J.: Unsupervised corpus aware language model pre-training for dense passage retrieval. arXiv preprint arXiv:2108.05540 (2021)
10. Guo, D., Yang, D., Zhang, H., Song, J., et al.: Deepseek-r1: incentivizing reasoning capability in LLMS via reinforcement learning. arXiv preprint arXiv:2501.12948 (2025)
11. Guo, J., Cai, Y., Fan, Y., Sun, F., Zhang, R., Cheng, X.: Semantic models for the first-stage retrieval: a comprehensive review. ACM Trans. Inf. Syst. (TOIS) **40**(4), 1–42 (2022)
12. Guo, J., Fan, Y., Ai, Q., Croft, W.B.: A deep relevance matching model for ad-hoc retrieval. In: Proceedings of the 25th ACM International on Conference on Information and Knowledge Management, pp. 55–64 (2016)
13. Hendrycks, D., Basart, S., Kadavath, S., Mazeika, M., et al.: Measuring coding challenge competence with apps. arXiv preprint arXiv:2105.09938 (2021)
14. Huang, J., Tang, D., Shou, L., et al.: Cosqa: 20,000+ web queries for code search and question answering. arXiv preprint arXiv:2105.13239 (2021)
15. Hui, B., Yang, J., Cui, Z., et al.: Qwen2. 5-coder technical report. arXiv preprint arXiv:2409.12186 (2024)
16. Husain, H., Wu, H.H., Gazit, T., Allamanis, M., Brockschmidt, M.: Codesearchnet challenge: evaluating the state of semantic code search. arXiv preprint arXiv:1909.09436 (2019)

17. Karpukhin, V., Oguz, B., Min, S., Lewis, P.S., et al.: Dense passage retrieval for open-domain question answering. In: EMNLP (1), pp. 6769–6781 (2020)
18. Li, C., Liu, Z., Xiao, S., Shao, Y., Lian, D.: Llama2vec: unsupervised adaptation of large language models for dense retrieval. In: Proceedings of the 62nd Annual Meeting of the Association for Computational Linguistics (Volume 1: Long Papers), pp. 3490–3500 (2024)
19. Li, X., Dong, K., Lee, Y.Q., Xia, W., et al.: Coir: a comprehensive benchmark for code information retrieval models. arXiv preprint arXiv:2407.02883 (2024)
20. Liu, A., Feng, B., Xue, B., et al.: Deepseek-v3 technical report. arXiv preprint arXiv:2412.19437 (2024)
21. Ma, X., Guo, J., Zhang, R., Fan, Y., Ji, X., Cheng, X.: Prop: pre-training with representative words prediction for ad-hoc retrieval. In: Proceedings of the 14th ACM International Conference on Web Search and Data Mining, pp. 283–291 (2021)
22. Ma, X., Wang, L., Yang, N., Wei, F., Lin, J.: Fine-tuning llama for multi-stage text retrieval. In: Proceedings of the 47th International ACM SIGIR Conference on Research and Development in Information Retrieval, pp. 2421–2425 (2024)
23. Maia, M., Handschuh, S., Freitas, A., Davis, B., et al.: Www'18 open challenge: financial opinion mining and question answering. In: Companion Proceedings of the Web Conference 2018, pp. 1941–1942 (2018)
24. Nguyen, T., Rosenberg, M., Song, X., Gao, J., Tiwary, S., Majumder, R., Deng, L.: Ms marco: a human-generated machine reading comprehension dataset (2016)
25. Qu, Y., Ding, Y., Liu, J., Liu, K., et al.: Rocketqa: an optimized training approach to dense passage retrieval for open-domain question answering. arXiv preprint arXiv:2010.08191 (2020)
26. Robertson, S., Zaragoza, H., et al.: The probabilistic relevance framework: Bm25 and beyond. Found. Trends® Inf. Retrieval **3**(4), 333–389 (2009)
27. Springer, J.M., Kotha, S., Fried, D., Neubig, G., Raghunathan, A.: Repetition improves language model embeddings. arXiv preprint arXiv:2402.15449 (2024)
28. Springer, J.M., Kotha, S., Fried, D., Neubig, G., Raghunathan, A.: Repetition improves language model embeddings. arXiv preprint arXiv:2402.15449 (2024)
29. Thakur, N., Reimers, N., Rücklé, A., Srivastava, A., Gurevych, I.: Beir: a heterogenous benchmark for zero-shot evaluation of information retrieval models. arXiv preprint arXiv:2104.08663 (2021)
30. Vaswani, A., Shazeer, N., Parmar, N., et al.: Attention is all you need. Adv. Neural Inf. Process. Syst. **30** (2017)
31. Wachsmuth, H., Syed, S., Stein, B.: Retrieval of the best counterargument without prior topic knowledge. In: Proceedings of the 56th Annual Meeting of the Association for Computational Linguistics (Volume 1: Long Papers), pp. 241–251 (2018)
32. Wang, L.L., Lo, K., Chandrasekhar, Y., Reas, R., et al.: Cord-19: the covid-19 open research dataset. ArXiv pp. arXiv–2004 (2020)
33. Xiao, S., Liu, Z., Shao, Y., Cao, Z.: Retromae: pre-training retrieval-oriented language models via masked auto-encoder. arXiv preprint arXiv:2205.12035 (2022)
34. Yan, W., Tian, Y., Li, Y., et al.: Codetransocean: a comprehensive multilingual benchmark for code translation. arXiv preprint arXiv:2310.04951 (2023)
35. Yang, A., Yang, B., Hui, B., et al.: Qwen2 technical report (2024)
36. Yang, A., Yang, B., Zhang, B., et al.: Qwen2.5 technical report (2025)
37. Yang, A., Zhang, B., Hui, B., et al.: Qwen2. 5-math technical report: Toward mathematical expert model via self-improvement. arXiv preprint arXiv:2409.12122 (2024)

38. Zhang, H., et al.: Unleashing the power of LLMS in dense retrieval with query likelihood modeling. arXiv preprint arXiv:2504.05216 (2025)
39. Zheng, T., Zhang, G., Shen, T., et al.: Opencodeinterpreter: integrating code generation with execution and refinement. arXiv preprint arXiv:2402.14658 (2024)
40. Zhuang, S., Ma, X., Koopman, B., Lin, J., Zuccon, G.: Promptreps: prompting large language models to generate dense and sparse representations for zero-shot document retrieval. arXiv preprint arXiv:2404.18424 (2024)

Generalizable and Robust Phenotypic Drug Discovery

Xin Hong[1], Jiaxin Zheng[2], Xingsi Xie[3], Yinjun Jia[1], Yuyan Ni[4,5], and Yanyan Lan[1,6(✉)]

[1] Institute for AI Industry Research (AIR), Tsinghua University, Beijing, China
{hongxin,jiayinjun,lanyanyan}@air.tsinghua.edu.cn
[2] College of Computer Science and Technology, Jilin University, Changchun, Jilin, China
zhengjx22@mails.jlu.edu.cn
[3] Department of Pharmaceutical Science, Peking University, Beijing, China
2110307329@stu.pku.edu.cn
[4] Academy of Mathematics and Systems Science, Chinese Academy of Sciences, Beijing, China
niyuyan17@mails.ucas.ac.cn
[5] University of Chinese Academy of Sciences, Beijing, China
[6] Beijing Academy of Artificial Intelligence (BAAI), Beijing, China

Abstract. Phenotypic virtual screening holds great promise for discovering therapeutic compounds by directly linking molecular effects to disease-relevant phenotypic outcomes. However, existing computational methods face critical limitations in generalizing across diverse biological contexts and mitigating experimental noise inherent in high-throughput screens. We present PhenotypeCLIP, a robust framework for phenotype-aware drug retrieval that integrates multi-modal representation learning and noise-invariant alignment. The framework leverages pretrained molecular encoders enriched with chemical property and protein target interaction knowledge to model compound-phenotype mechanisms, while explicitly capturing the interplay between molecules and baseline cellular states through latent variable modeling. An information bottleneck further enforces noise-robust representations by prioritizing predictive signals over batch-specific artifacts. Evaluated on cell line-stratified LINCS datasets, PhenotypeCLIP achieves a 3.85-fold improvement in top-1 retrieval recall on unseen cell lines compared to state-of-the-art methods and demonstrates superior few-shot learning performance in mechanism-of-action prediction and drug response prediction. These advancements establish a new paradigm for generalizable and interpretable phenotypic drug discovery, bridging molecular mechanisms with systemic therapeutic effects.

X. Hong and J. Zheng—Equal contribution.

Z. Li et al. (Eds.): CCIR 2025, LNCS 16369, pp. 62–75, 2026.
https://doi.org/10.1007/978-981-95-5637-3_5

1 Introduction

Drug discovery can be viewed as a retrieval problem, where the goal is to identify bioactive molecules from large chemical libraries using disease-related signals, such as protein targets or phenotypic profiles. Traditionally, target-based virtual screening (TBVS) has dominated this space by retrieving molecules that bind to predefined molecular targets, such as disease-associated proteins [17]. In recent years, there has been a growing shift toward phenotypic virtual screening (PVS), which retrieves molecules based on their ability to reverse disease-relevant phenotypes, e.g. abnormal cell proliferation or metabolic dysfunction. This trend is supported by an analysis of FDA-approved drugs, showing that between 1999 and 2008, phenotypic approaches produced 40% more first-in-class drugs than TBVS, with 28 versus 17 approvals [19]. PVS bypasses the need for predefined target hypotheses by directly linking molecular candidates to functional disease phenotypes, such as tumor regression or immune modulation [20]. This approach avoids dependence on incomplete or ambiguous target annotations and better aligns retrieval objectives with clinically meaningful outcomes, capturing systemic effects that TBVS often overlooks [11]. Thus, a critical direction is to leverage the experience and methodologies from target-based virtual screening to develop effective phenotypic virtual screening approaches.

Recent advances in bulk and single-cell profiling technologies [8] have significantly expanded the availability of high-dimensional phenotypic data, e.g. LINCS [18] and Cell Painting [2], enabling the development of computational models that predict molecular-induced phenotypic changes. Approaches like InfoCORE [23] and InfoAlign [9] leverage contrastive learning to align chemical structures with gene expression perturbations. Despite their success in modeling compound-phenotype relationships, these methods face critical limitations stemming from data constraints. Existing datasets lack sufficient coverage across diverse cell lines and chemical space, limiting their ability to generalize to novel cellular environments or compounds. Furthermore, experimental noise from batch effects and technical variability obscures true compound-phenotype interactions, complicating the training of reliable models [4]. Addressing these challenges of sparse biological and chemical representation alongside persistent measurement noise remains essential for advancing robust phenotypic virtual screening.

In this paper, we propose PhenotypeCLIP, a novel framework that enhances phenotypic virtual screening by integrating multi-modal contrastive learning with robust training strategies. The framework first incorporates a pretrained molecular encoder from DrugCLIP [3], which enhances chemical representation by aligning molecules with both structural properties and protein targets through contrastive learning. This dual alignment captures general chemical features and target interaction mechanisms critical for phenotype modulation, thereby enriching molecular representations for phenotypic prediction. Additionally, unlike existing methods that directly map compounds to phenotypic shifts, PhenotypeCLIP models latent variables encoding the combined effects of compounds and baseline cellular states, enabling context-aware prediction of phenotype changes.

Furthermore, to mitigate experimental noise, the framework employs an information bottleneck [1,21] that optimizes latent variables to discard irrelevant input noise while preserving predictive signals for phenotypic outcomes. By unifying these innovations, PhenotypeCLIP advances generalizable and robust phenotypic compound retrieval across diverse biological contexts.

We evaluate PhenotypeCLIP on the LINCS dataset [18] using a cell line-stratified split to rigorously assess its generalization to unseen cellular contexts. In the phenotypic virtual screening task, PhenotypeCLIP achieves a top-1 recall rate 385% higher than state-of-the-art baselines (from 7.76% to 37.20%), demonstrating superior accuracy in identifying bioactive molecules that reverse disease-relevant phenotypes. Furthermore, when adapting to downstream mechanism of action (MOA) prediction and drug response prediction via few-shot fine-tuning, our framework outperforms existing methods, highlighting its transferability across tasks with limited labeled data. Ablation studies confirm the contributions of its core components: pretraining on molecular-target interactions enhanced its capacity to infer phenotype-modulating mechanisms, while joint modeling of baseline phenotypes and compound effects improved context specificity. The information bottleneck further reduced sensitivity to batch effects, with noise-robust representations yielding consistent performance across experimental replicates. These results collectively establish PhenotypeCLIP as a generalizable and robust solution for phenotypic virtual screening.

The main contributions of our work can be summarized as follows:

- We present the first computational framework that systematically models the mechanistic interplay between small molecules and phenotypic changes. This is achieved by integrating molecular representations pretrained on chemical properties and protein target interactions, enabling comprehensive modeling of phenotype-modulating mechanisms.
- We develop an information bottleneck mechanism to reduce the impact of experimental noise (e.g., batch effects) and observational errors in high-throughput screens. This approach learns noise-invariant representations by minimizing mutual information between latent variables and noisy inputs while preserving predictive signals.
- We demonstrate through rigorous cell line-stratified experiments that PhenotypeCLIP achieves state-of-the-art performance in phenotypic virtual screening. The framework shows a 385% improvement in top-1 retrieval accuracy on unseen cell lines compared to existing methods (from 7.76% to 37.20%), along with superior few-shot learning capabilities for mechanism-of-action prediction and drug response prediction.

2 Related Work

Traditional drug discovery efforts have long relied on target-based approaches, which have achieved remarkable success in the past decades by focusing on well-characterized protein structures [26]. However, this strategy faces inherent limitations when applied to diseases lacking clearly defined molecular targets, prompting a paradigm shift toward phenotype-based virtual screening [12]. Phenotype-based screening aims to identify bioactive compounds by analyzing measurable cellular responses, such as gene expression profiles or morphological changes. The central challenge lies in achieving robust generalization, particularly when predicting the effects of novel compounds or cell lines absent from training data, such as those in widely used datasets like L1000 [18].To address this, diverse computational methods have emerged, each rooted in distinct hypotheses about how small molecules mechanistically influence gene expression dynamics.

A fundamental strategy for modeling drug-induced transcriptional changes involves directly predicting gene expression profiles from molecular structures, as implemented in DLEPS [27], which trains a deep neural network to predict drug-induced transcriptional profiles from chemical representations. In parallel, methods like InfoCORE [23] enhance robustness to experimental artifacts by employing contrastive learning to disentangle biological signals from batch effects, optimizing latent representations through mutual information maximization while adaptively balancing batch-specific distributions.

Approaches that directly model small molecule-transcriptional response relationships often neglect the basal state's crucial role in modulating drug response variability. Recent advances integrate basal gene expression profiles with molecular representations to enhance perturbation modeling. PRnet [15] combines chemical structures and cellular contexts in a deep generative framework for predicting novel compound responses, achieving cross-tissue generalization and enabling gene-level interpretation. TranSiGen [22] jointly encodes basal expression and molecular features through self-supervised learning, improving drug repurposing and phenotype screening accuracy. ChemCPA [5] bridges bulk and single-cell data via transfer learning, using bulk RNA perturbation data to predict unseen drug effects at single-cell resolution, effectively reducing experimental costs.

Existing approaches often fail to mechanistically explain how small molecules initiate cellular state transitions, limiting their utility for novel compounds or cell types. Recent methods address this by integrating biological network priors. For example, DeepCE [14] uses a graph neural network with multihead attention to model chemical-gene and gene-gene interactions, enabling de novo gene expression prediction. Similarly, MultiDCP [24] employs a knowledge-driven transformer to predict context-dependent expression and dose-responsive viability, transferring patterns from bulk to single-cell data. GEARS [16] improves multigene perturbation prediction by embedding Gene Ontology relationships, inferring outcomes for untested gene combinations.

Recent advances in molecular pretraining frameworks, such as UniMol [25], encode chemically meaningful features from vast unlabeled datasets—knowledge inherently absent in small-scale, labeled perturbation datasets like L1000. While models like DrugCLIP [25] further align these representations with protein interaction mechanisms to reflect regulatory pathways, existing methods for predicting transcriptional responses underutilize such pretrained knowledge. Our work integrates these enriched molecular embeddings to address generalization chal-

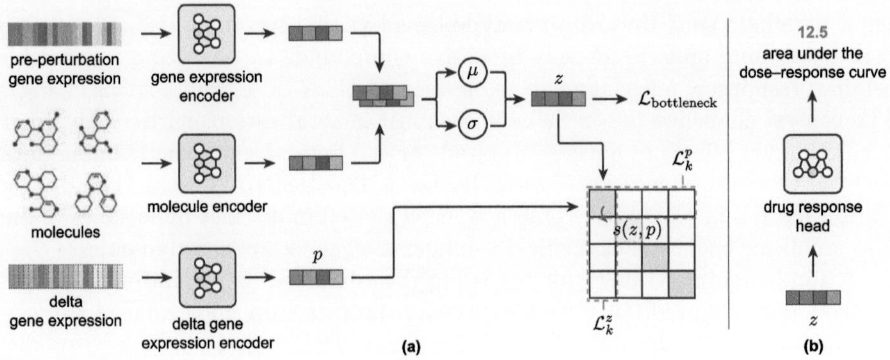

Fig. 1. Illustration of the PhenotypeCLIP. **(a)** The training procedure of PhenotypeCLIP. **(b)** Drug response prediction based on pretrained PhenotypeCLIP.

lenges in drug-induced gene expression modeling, particularly for novel compounds or contexts where mechanistic annotations are sparse. By bridging pretrained chemical insights with perturbation-specific learning, we aim to transcend the limitations of data scarcity and enhance robustness across diverse biological systems.

3 Methods

3.1 Overview

The phenotypic virtual screening (PVS) is a retrieval problem, wherein the objective is to identify candidate small molecules capable of eliciting a desired gene expression change within a specific cellular context. Let x represent the pre-perturbation transcriptomic profile of a cell, capturing its basal state. Upon treatment with a molecule m, the cellular state transitions to a post-perturbation expression profile x'. The induced transcriptomic shift is quantified by the differential expression:

$$\Delta x = x' - x,$$

which reflects the molecule-specific perturbation relative to the baseline. Given a target post-perturbation expression profile x' and its associated pre-perturbation state x, PVS aims to efficiently rank and retrieve the top-k molecules from a candidate library $\mathcal{M} = \{m_1, m_2, \ldots, m_n\}$ (containing n molecules) that are predicted to most closely reproduce the differential expression Δx.

We frame phenotypic virtual screening as a dense retrieval task by leveraging differential expression to align small molecule perturbations with their effects on the pre-perturbation state. Figure 1 illustrates the PhenotypeCLIP framework. Three encoders are trained independently to learn representations of the differential expression, the pre-perturbation profile, and the molecule. These representations are then fused to generate a context-aware perturbation representation z. A contrastive learning objective aligns this representation with the target differential expression, allowing the model to differentiate between positive and negative pairs.

3.2 Multi-Modal Encoders

To model the complex relationship between molecular perturbations and cellular phenotypes, PhenotypeCLIP incorporates a set of modality-specific encoders that extract informative representations from both molecular structures and gene expression profiles. These encoders serve as the foundational components for capturing how small molecules interact with cellular systems to produce specific transcriptional outcomes.

Molecular Encoder. To address the limited coverage of small molecules in phenotypic screening training data, we incorporate the pretrained molecular encoder $f_{\text{mol}}(\cdot)$ from DrugCLIP [3], a contrastive learning framework initially developed for target-based virtual screening. This encoder, built on the Uni-Mol [25] architecture, learns universal 3D molecular representations through self-supervised pretraining on two tasks, including 3D position recovery and masked atom prediction—enabling it to capture molecular properties across physical and biochemical scales. In DrugCLIP, the encoder is further fine-tuned via contrastive learning to align molecular embeddings with protein target representations, thereby acquiring knowledge of drug-target interaction patterns. Although our task does not explicitly involve protein inputs, this pretraining allows the encoder to implicitly model functional relationships relevant to cellular perturbation, combining both structural and interaction-aware features. The input of the encoder includes the molecule's 3D coordinates as well as its atom types. As for the 3D coordinates, we generate multiple 3D conformers for each molecule m_i, and randomly select one to obtain the corresponding coordinates.

Gene Expression Encoders. While the molecular encoder captures the properties of the perturbing compound, modeling the cellular phenotype requires understanding both the pre-existing cellular state and its transcriptional response. To this end, we introduce two gene expression encoders, including a pre-perturbation gene expression encoder $f_\phi(\cdot)$ and a delta gene expression encoder $g_\phi(\cdot)$. Both process 978-dimensional vectors representing landmark gene expression levels, extracting features relevant to perturbation effects. The pre-perturbation encoder f_ϕ captures the cellular context before before perturbation, while g_ϕ focuses on the induced expression changes. Together, they enable PhenotypeCLIP to comprehensively represent the cellular state in response to molecular perturbation. These encoders can be implemented in various ways, such as using untrained multilayer perceptrons (MLPs) or pretrained variational autoencoders (VAEs). However, we found that even a few layers of MLPs suffice to achieve competitive performance.

3.3 Contrastive Learning Objective

In the context of phenotypic virtual screening, our goal is to model the perturbational effects of small molecules on cellular states. To measure the relevance between fused representations z and post-perturbation profiles, we adopt the dot product as the similarity function. Specifically, the similarity between the context-aware perturbation embedding z^k, fused from pre-perturbation representation and moleculear representation, and a post-perturbation embedding $p_i = g_\phi(\Delta x^i)$ is defined as:

$$s(z_k, p_i) = z_k \cdot p_i. \tag{1}$$

Given a batch of N paired samples $\{((m_k, x^k), \Delta x^k)\}_{k=1}^N$, we first obtain their corresponding representation pairs $\{(z_k, p_k)\}_{k=1}^N$, and then construct contrastive pairs by treaing all diagonal pairs (z_k, p_i) as positives and all off-diagonal pairs (z_k, p_i) where $i \neq k$ as negatives. Each molecule induces a unique perturbation signature, such that mismatched molecule-state combinations are unlikely to be biologically relevant.

The similarity scores are normalized through softmax to compute two contrastive losses. The first optimizes the fused embedding z_k to match its corresponding post-perturbation embedding p_k:

$$\mathcal{L}_k^z = -\log \frac{\exp(z_k \cdot p_k/\tau)}{\sum_{i=1}^N \exp(z_k \cdot p_i/\tau)}, \tag{2}$$

where τ is a temperature hyperparameter that controls the sharpness of the softmax distribution. The second loss ensures post-perturbation embedding p_k selectively aligns with its context-aware perturbation embedding z_k:

$$\mathcal{L}_k^p = -\log \frac{\exp(z_k \cdot p_k/\tau)}{\sum_{i=1}^N \exp(z_i \cdot p_k/\tau)}. \tag{3}$$

Combining the two losses, we obtain the final loss for a batch of N paired samples:

$$\mathcal{L}_{\text{contrast}} = \frac{1}{2N} \sum_{k=1}^{N} (\mathcal{L}_k^z + \mathcal{L}_k^p). \tag{4}$$

This bidirectional contrastive objective encourages the model to learn perturbation-relevant features, enabling accurate alignment of molecular effects with their phenotypic outcomes and facilitating generalization across unseen compounds and cellular contexts.

3.4 Robust Training

Modeling transcriptomic responses to molecular perturbations presents a fundamental challenge in distinguishing biologically meaningful signals from confounding noise. This noise encompasses both technical artifacts such as batch effects and inherent biological variability across cell lines. Unregularized models risk overfitting to these nuisance factors, resulting in spurious correlations and compromised generalizability. To enhance robustness, we employ a dual approach combining the Information Bottleneck (IB) principle [1,21] and a carefully designed cell line-constrained batch sampling strategy. The Information Bottleneck enforces biologically relevant feature extraction while the sampling strategy mitigates technical artifacts while preserving biological diversity.

Information Bottleneck. Our framework implements the Information Bottleneck principle to derive compressed yet biologically meaningful representations of perturbation effects. The process begins by concatenating the molecular descriptor $f_{\text{mol}}(m_i)$ with the pre-perturbation transcriptomic state $f_\phi(x)$, forming a composite input $[f_{\text{mol}}(m_i); f_\phi(x)]$. This combined representation undergoes transformation through a variational encoder, which outputs parameters for a diagonal Gaussian distribution $\mathcal{N}(\boldsymbol{\mu}, \text{diag}(\boldsymbol{\sigma}^2))$. The final latent representation z is then sampled from this distribution using the reparameterization trick, ensuring differentiability during training:

$$z = \boldsymbol{\mu} + \boldsymbol{\sigma} \odot \boldsymbol{\epsilon}, \quad \boldsymbol{\epsilon} \sim \mathcal{N}(0, \mathbf{I}). \tag{5}$$

To prevent z from capturing irrelevant variations in the input, we impose an information bottleneck regularization term to minimize the mutual information between the latent representation and the input. Based on the variational approximation in [1], this mutual information is upper-bounded by the learned posterior and a standard normal prior. The bottleneck loss is defined as:

$$\begin{aligned} \mathcal{L}_{\text{bottleneck}} &= \frac{1}{N}\sum_{k=1}^{N} D_{\text{KL}}\left(\mathcal{N}(\boldsymbol{\mu}^k, \text{diag}((\boldsymbol{\sigma}^k)^2)) \,\|\, \mathcal{N}(0, \mathbf{I})\right) \\ &= \frac{1}{2N}\sum_{k=1}^{N}\sum_{j=1}^{d}\left({\mu_j^k}^2 + {\sigma_j^k}^2 - \log {\sigma_j^k}^2 - 1\right) \end{aligned} \tag{6}$$

This encourages the latent space to capture only information essential for predicting post-perturbation expression, while filtering out context-specific noise such as batch effects.

To jointly optimize the contrastive learning objective and the information bottleneck regularization, we combine the contrastive loss with the KL divergence term, weighted by β that controls the strength of the regularization:

$$\mathcal{L}_{\text{final}} = \mathcal{L}_{\text{contrast}} + \beta\mathcal{L}_{\text{bottleneck}}. \tag{7}$$

This total loss balances the alignment of molecular effects with phenotypic outcomes (via $\mathcal{L}_{\text{contrast}}$) and the compression of the latent representation to retain only task-relevant information (via the KL term), enabling robust generalization across diverse compounds and cellular contexts.

Table 1. Performance on the phenotype-molecule retrieval task.

Top-k Recall(%)	k=1	k=5	k=10
TranSiGen	1.09	5.83	11.20
InfoCORE	7.67	21.94	31.61
PhenotypeCLIP	**37.20**	**77.71**	**87.28**

Cell Line-Constrained Batch Sampling. Inspired by InfoCORE [23], we adopt a structured batch sampling strategy during training, where each mini-batch consists exclusively of samples from a single cell line. This design ensures a consistent cellular background within each batch, thereby reducing cross-cell line variability and preventing the model from relying on cell line identity as a shortcut for prediction. By controlling for cellular context in this way, the model is compelled to focus on perturbation-driven features rather than cell lineâĂŞspecific patterns, promoting the learning of generalizable representations across diverse biological conditions.

4 Experiments

To validate the advantages of PhenotypeCLIP, we evaluate our model on the common used phenotype virtual screening dataset. We also show Phenotype-CLIP performs well on related downstream tasks including mechanism of action (MOA) prediction and drug response prediction. Finally, an ablation study is conducted to assess the contributions of key components in PhenotypeCLIP.

4.1 Setup

Dataset. We employ the LINCS dataset [7,18], a high-throughput drug perturbation resource, aligning with the preprocessing methodology of TranSiGen [22] to ensure consistency with prior work. This dataset provides transcriptional profiles of 978 landmark genes, where each observation consists of a molecule and the paired gene expression measurements, including the pre-perturbed gene expression x and its corresponding post-perturbed gene expression x'. We following TransiGen preprocessing on the data, yielding a consolidated dataset of 78,569 perturbation pairs spanning 8,316 compounds and 164 cell lines. To evaluate how PhenotypeCLIP generalize to unseen cellular contexts, we partition the dataset into training, validation, and test sets based on cell lines.

Implementation Detail. We adopt two separate multi-layer perceptron (MLP) encoders for pre-perturbation gene expression and delta gene expression, consists of two fully connected layers and a dropout rate of 0.1. Both encoders operate on 978-dimensional gene expression input vectors. PhenotypeCLIP is trained using the AdamW [10] optimizer with a learning rate of 1e-4. We have a batch size of 256, using 4 NVIDIA A100 GPU for acceleration. PyTorch [6] is used as the primary deep learning framework and the Hydra configuration system is used for experiment management. To balance the contrastive alignment and information bottleneck regularization, we set the weight coefficient β to 1e-5.

4.2 Phenotypic Virtual Screening

Phenotypic virtual screening constitutes a retrieval task that identifies candidate small molecules capable of inducing observed transcriptional shifts between paired pre-perturbed and post-perturbed gene expression.

Metrics. Performance is evaluated via top-k recall ($k = 1, 5, 10$), which quantifies the success rate of retrieving the true molecules within the top-k candidates.

Results. As shown in Table 1, PhenotypeCLIP demonstrates superior performance compared to state-of-the-art baseline methods, including InfoCORE [23]and TranSiGen [22]. Notably, PhenotypeCLIP achieves a remarkable 385% improvement in Top-1 recall over InfoCORE (from 7.76% to 37.20%), highlighting its exceptional capability in phenotype-molecule retrieval. We posit that this performance gain primarily stems from our integration of a molecular encoder with stronger biological priors. By leveraging limited drug perturbation data, the model effectively captures the relationship between small molecules and gene expression patterns. Crucially, when encountering novel cell lines and compounds, the system demonstrates robust generalization capabilities by building upon both large-scale molecular pretraining and protein-binding knowledge. This dual foundation enables reliable inference even for previously unseen biological contexts.

4.3 Mechanism of Action Prediction Task

Mechanism-of-Action (MoA) prediction is the task of identifying how a drug molecule exerts its biological effects by modulating specific protein targets. The input is a small molecule (drug candidate), and the output is its predicted MoA label, which describes its functional impact on biological pathways.

Metrics. The evaluation employs standard classification metrics, including precision for positive predictive value, recall for true positive rate, and F1-score as their harmonic mean. Both micro and macro versions are reported, where micro averaging weights by instance frequency and macro averaging treats all classes equally to ensure robust evaluation across imbalanced MoA categories.

Table 2. Performance comparison on the MoA prediction task.

Model	Precision		Recall		F1	
	Micro	Macro	Micro	Macro	Micro	Macro
Uni-Mol	0.4772	0.4388	0.4772	0.4792	0.4772	0.4446
DrugCLIP	0.5742	0.5728	0.5742	0.5367	0.5742	0.6144
PhenotypeCLIP	**0.6355**	**0.6508**	**0.6533**	**0.6359**	**0.6355**	**0.6126**

Table 3. Performance comparison on drug response prediction

Model	RMSE ↓	Pearson ↑	R^2 ↑
CIGER	3.926 ± 0.016	−0.074 ± 0.015	−0.153 ± 0.010
DLEPS	3.825 ± 0.045	0.122 ± 0.023	−0.094 ± 0.026
DeepCE	3.908 ± 0.042	−0.069 ± 0.044	−0.142 ± 0.025
TranSiGen	3.094 ± 0.022	**0.574 ± 0.016**	0.284 ± 0.010
PhenotypeCLIP	**3.075 ± 0.012**	0.557 ± 0.006	**0.293 ± 0.006**

Results. We compare two strong molecular pretraining models, Uni-Mol [25] and DrugCLIP [3], as baselines. All three models share an identical architecture where fixed molecular encoders are coupled with multilayer perceptron heads, fine-tuned on limited MoA-labeled data for this regression prediction task before evaluation. Uni-Mol employs solely unsupervised pretraining on molecular structures and demonstrates the weakest performance. DrugCLIP, building upon Uni-Mol's foundation, additionally incorporates protein-ligand interaction knowledge, which provides more relevant signals since MoAs fundamentally arise from molecular modulation of protein targets. However, as shown in Table 2, our proposed PhenotypeCLIP surpasses both approaches by directly learning from drug perturbation data. Since gene expression changes constitute phenotypic manifestations closely aligned with MoA outcomes, this training paradigm enables PhenotypeCLIP to achieve superior predictive performance on MoA classification tasks. This performance hierarchy indirectly demonstrates that phenotype-based virtual screening may yield more therapeutically relevant compounds than traditional target-based approaches, as it directly optimizes for desired treatment effects at the phenotypic level rather than through presumed target modulation.

4.4 Drug Response Prediction

Drug response prediction is a task that estimates a drug's effect on cell viability by predicting the area under the dose-response curve (AUC). The input combines drug molecular features and the gene expression of the basal state, while the output predicts the AUC value where lower scores indicate stronger growth inhibition potential.

Table 4. Ablation Studies on Mechanism Modeling and Robust Training

Method	k=1	k=5	k=10
Mechanism Modeling			
PhenotypeCLIP (w/o pre-perturbation)	26.75	62.65	75.62
PhenotypeCLIP (w/o DrugCLIP)	**38.13**	71.40	87.00
Robust Training			
PhenotypeCLIP (w/o IB)	36.36	74.77	87.69
PhenotypeCLIP (w/o sampling strategy)	28.29	70.13	85.49
PhenotypeCLIP (full model)	37.20	**77.71**	**87.28**

Metrics. Drug response prediction performance is assessed through three key metrics. RMSE quantifies prediction errors while Pearson correlation evaluates linear relationships between predicted and actual values. R^2 measures how well the model explains data variance. Better models demonstrate lower RMSE values alongside higher Pearson correlation and R^2 scores.

Results. We compared CIGER [13], DLEPS [27], DeepCE [14], and TranSiGen [22] on the drug response prediction task. The results from Table 3 demonstrate that PhenotypeCLIP achieves superior performance compared to all baseline methods, with TransiGen showing relatively close performance. This similarity arises because the test cell lines, despite being finetuned with limited labeled data, were already covered during training, and both PhenotypeCLIP and TranSiGen effectively model the relationship between cell lines and small molecules. Other methods exhibit weaker performance due to less comprehensive mechanism modeling. However, additional experiments reveal that PhenotypeCLIP's key advantage lies in its generalization capability, particularly its strong performance on unseen cell lines where it significantly outperforms all other approaches Table 4.

4.5 Ablation Study

The ablation studies demonstrate key insights into PhenotypeCLIP's performance. First, modeling the relationship between small molecules and gene expression profiles benefits significantly from incorporating pre-perturbation gene expression as input rather than relying solely on delta gene expression, which proves crucial for phenotypic virtual screening accuracy. While integrating DrugCLIP weights provides moderate recall improvements, the model's generalization capability primarily stems from UniMol's comprehensive small molecule property learning. Regarding robustness, the information bottleneck technique and cell line-based sampling strategy collectively enhance model stability, enabling PhenotypeCLIP to maintain consistent performance across different evaluation scenarios. The full model achieves optimal results by synergistically combining these mechanistic modeling and robust training components.

5 Conclusion

PhenotypeCLIP significantly advances phenotypic virtual screening by effectively modeling small molecule-gene expression relationships while ensuring robustness to experimental noise. Extensive experiments on the LINCS dataset demonstrate its superior performance, achieving a 3.85-fold improvement in top-1 retrieval accuracy over state-of-the-art methods for unseen cell lines while also showing leading results in mechanism-of-action prediction and drug response forecasting. The model's success stems from its novel approach to mechanistic modeling that captures pre-perturbation cellular states alongside molecular properties, combined with robust training techniques including information bottleneck and cell line-aware sampling. Ablation studies confirm both components are critical for the model's strong generalization capabilities. These advances establish PhenotypeCLIP as a new reference framework for phenotypic drug discovery that bridges molecular mechanisms with therapeutic effects.

Acknowledgment. This work is supported by Beijing Academy of Artificial Intelligence (BAAI).

References

1. Alemi, A.A., Fischer, I., Dillon, J.V., Murphy, K.: Deep variational information bottleneck. In: International Conference on Learning Representations (2017)
2. Bray, M.A., et al.: Cell Painting, a high-content image-based assay for morphological profiling using multiplexed fluorescent dyes. Nat. Protoc. **11**(9), 1757–1774 (2016). https://doi.org/10.1038/nprot.2016.105
3. Gao, B., et al.: DrugCLIP: contrastive protein-molecule representation learning for virtual screening (2023). https://doi.org/10.48550/arXiv.2310.06367
4. Goh, W.W.B., Wang, W., Wong, L.: Why batch effects matter in omics data, and how to avoid them. Trends Biotechnol. **35**(6), 498–507 (2017)
5. Hetzel, L., Böhm, S., Kilbertus, N., Günnemann, S., Lotfollahi, M., Theis, F.: Predicting cellular responses to novel drug perturbations at a single-cell resolution (2022). https://doi.org/10.48550/arXiv.2204.13545
6. Imambi, S., Prakash, K.B., Kanagachidambaresan, G.: Pytorch. Programming with TensorFlow: solution for edge computing applications, pp. 87–104 (2021)
7. Institute, B.: Expanded cmap lincs resource 2020. (2020). https://clue.io/data/CMap2020#LINCS2020, Accessed 20 Feb 2022
8. Li, X., Wang, C.Y.: From bulk, single-cell to spatial RNA sequencing. Int. J. Oral Sci. **13**(1), 1–6 (2021)
9. Liu, G., Seal, S., Arevalo, J., Liang, Z., Carpenter, A.E., Jiang, M., Singh, S.: Learning molecular representation in a cell (2024). https://doi.org/10.48550/arXiv.2406.12056
10. Loshchilov, I., Hutter, F.: Decoupled weight decay regularization. arXiv preprint arXiv:1711.05101 (2017)
11. Moffat, J.G., Vincent, F., Lee, J.A., Eder, J., Prunotto, M.: Opportunities and challenges in phenotypic drug discovery: An industry perspective. Nat. Rev. Drug Discovery **16**(8), 531–543 (2017). https://doi.org/10.1038/nrd.2017.111

12. Moshkov, N., et al.: Predicting compound activity from phenotypic profiles and chemical structures. Nat. Commun. **14**(1), 1967 (2023)
13. Pham, T.H., et al.: Chemical-induced gene expression ranking and its application to pancreatic cancer drug repurposing. Patterns **3**(4), 100441 (2022). https://doi.org/10.1016/j.patter.2022.100441
14. Pham, T.H., Qiu, Y., Zeng, J., Xie, L., Zhang, P.: A deep learning framework for high-throughput mechanism-driven phenotype compound screening and its application to COVID-19 drug repurposing. Nat. Mach. Intell. **3**(3), 247–257 (2021). https://doi.org/10.1038/s42256-020-00285-9
15. Qi, X., et al.: Predicting transcriptional responses to novel chemical perturbations using deep generative model for drug discovery. Nat. Commun. **15**(1), 9256 (2024). https://doi.org/10.1038/s41467-024-53457-1
16. Roohani, Y., Huang, K., Leskovec, J.: Predicting transcriptional outcomes of novel multigene perturbations with GEARS. Nat. Biotechnol. **42**(6), 927–935 (2024). https://doi.org/10.1038/s41587-023-01905-6
17. Sams-Dodd, F.: Target-based drug discovery: is something wrong? Drug Discovery Today **10**(2), 139–147 (2005)
18. Subramanian, A., et al.: A next generation connectivity map: L1000 platform and the first 1,000,000 profiles. Cell **171**(6), 1437-1452.e17 (2017). https://doi.org/10.1016/j.cell.2017.10.049
19. Swinney, D.C., Anthony, J.: How were new medicines discovered? Nat. Rev. Drug Discovery **10**(7), 507–519 (2011). https://doi.org/10.1038/nrd3480
20. Swinney, D.: Phenotypic vs. target-based drug discovery for first-in-class medicines. Clinical Pharmacol. Therapeutics **93**(4), 299–301 (2013)
21. Tishby, N., Pereira, F.C., Bialek, W.: The information bottleneck method. arXiv preprint physics/0004057 (2000)
22. Tong, X., et al.: Deep representation learning of chemical-induced transcriptional profile for phenotype-based drug discovery. Nat. Commun. **15**(1), 5378 (2024). https://doi.org/10.1038/s41467-024-49620-3
23. Wang, C., Gupta, S., Uhler, C., Jaakkola, T.: Removing biases from molecular representations via information maximization (2023). https://doi.org/10.48550/arXiv.2312.00718
24. Wu, Y., Liu, Q., Qiu, Y., Xie, L.: Deep learning prediction of chemical-induced dose-dependent and context-specific multiplex phenotype responses and its application to personalized alzheimer's disease drug repurposing. PLoS Comput. Biol. **18**(8), e1010367 (2022). https://doi.org/10.1371/journal.pcbi.1010367
25. Zhou, G., et al.: Uni-mol: a universal 3D molecular representation learning framework (2023). https://doi.org/10.26434/chemrxiv-2022-jjm0j-v4
26. Zhu, H., Zhang, Y., Li, W., Huang, N.: A comprehensive survey of prospective structure-based virtual screening for early drug discovery in the past fifteen years. Int. J. Molecular Sci. **23**(24), 15961 (2022)
27. Zhu, J., et al.: Prediction of drug efficacy from transcriptional profiles with deep learning. Nat. Biotechnol. **39**(11), 1444–1452 (2021). https://doi.org/10.1038/s41587-021-00946-z

FRAUDLLM: Zero-Shot Fraud Detection with Large Language Models

Mingyang An, Yuan Gao(✉), Jinghan Li, Xiang Wang, and Xiangnan He

University of Science and Technology of China, Hefei, China
{myan0423,yuanga,ljh111}@mail.ustc.edu.cn

Abstract. Graph-based fraud detection has emerged as a crucial technique for identifying anomalous patterns and suspicious behaviors across various domains, including financial transactions, e-commerce, and cybersecurity. However, existing methods predominantly rely on substantial labeled data for training, limiting their effectiveness in real-world scenarios where labels are scarce. Leveraging the exceptional zero-shot reasoning and instruction-following capabilities of Large Language Models (LLMs), we propose FRAUDLLM: **F**raud **R**easoning and **A**nomaly Detection via **U**nified **D**esign with **L**arge **L**anguage **M**odels, a novel zero-shot fraud detection framework. Specifically, it first generates semantic-rich text-graph pairs based on node metadata. Then, a pretrained text-graph aligner is employed to bridge the representation gap between the graph encoder and the text space of the LLM. Additionally, an in-context learning framework is designed to enable the LLM to effectively understand complex graph structures, significantly improving fraud detection performance in zero-shot scenarios without relying on labeled neighbor information. Extensive experiments on real-world datasets demonstrate that FRAUDLLM achieves state-of-the-art performance in zero-shot fraud detection tasks.

Keywords: Zero-Shot Fraud Detection · Graph Neural Network · Large Language Models

1 Introduction

With the rapid advancement of the Internet and digital technologies, online fraud has emerged as a critical global concern, encompassing various malicious activities such as fake reviews, fraudulent accounts, and deceptive websites. This phenomenon poses significant threats to e-commerce [8,13,27], financial transactions [10,15,24], and social media [1,26] platforms. In recent years, Graph Neural Networks (GNNs) [11,20,21] have gained considerable traction in the field of fraud detection. Through iterative message passing and representation learning, GNNs effectively aggregate neighborhood information, enabling the identification of anomalous or fraudulent entities based on enriched graph context.

To prevent themselves from being detected by the system, fraudsters disguise themselves in different ways, including emulating the features of benign

Z. Li et al. (Eds.): CCIR 2025, LNCS 16369, pp. 76–89, 2026.
https://doi.org/10.1007/978-981-95-5637-3_6

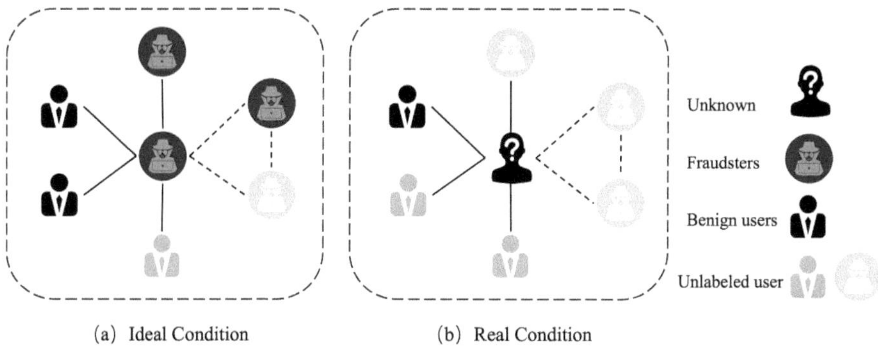

Fig. 1. A toy example illustrating the limitation of label-dependent fraud detection. Traditional methods rely heavily on a certain proportion of labeled neighboring nodes. However, in real-world scenarios, most neighboring nodes are unlabeled, making it difficult to uncover the camouflage of fraudsters

users (feature camouflage) and manipulating the graph structure by connecting to multiple benign users (structural camouflage) [4,7]. Fraudsters' camouflage behavior breaks the homophily assumption of GNN, so existing GNN-based research usually focuses on solving the camouflage problem in fraud detection. [4] adaptively selects the best neighbors for aggregation concerning arbitrarily many relationships, [5,18,23] propose to determine whether an edge represents a homogeneous or heterogeneous interaction, [22,25,28] argue that the use of node neighbor labels is more effective in identifying the type of relationship, and they embed the labeling information into the node representations or create label-aware embeddings, [9] uses MLP to generate pseudo-labels for nodes, and use different message passing and aggregation strategies depending on the fraud probability of the neighbors.

All of the above fraud detection methods utilize a large proportion of samples for training and validation, and heavily depend on labeled information. However, obtaining labels in graph-structured data under fraud scenarios is highly resource-intensive. In real-world settings, labels associated with fraudulent nodes are extremely sparse, as illustrated in Fig. 1, and conventional GNN-based approaches struggle to detect camouflaged fraudsters in the absence of sufficiently labeled neighborhoods. Therefore, it is imperative to develop methods that can effectively identify camouflage behaviors with minimal or even no supervision.

With the advancement of foundation models, Large Language Models have demonstrated impressive capabilities in understanding graph-related tasks [2, 19], particularly in zero-shot classification on text-attributed graphs. This offers new opportunities for fraud detection in low-resource settings, where labeled data is scarce. However, leveraging LLMs for graph-based fraud detection remains challenging due to three key limitations: (1) Modality gap: LLMs process sequential text tokens, while graph neural networks handle structured node-link data, making it challenging to capture complex topological and relational dependencies using text alone. (2) Alignment data scarcity: Effective integration of LLMs with graph data requires large-scale, well-aligned textual-structural pairs, which are costly to annotate and difficult to obtain across varied domains. (3) Fraud-specific challenges: Zero-shot fraud detection demands identifying subtle behavioral and structural anomalies without labeled data, placing high requirements on the model's reasoning and generalization abilities.

To overcome the above challenges, we propose FRAUDLLM, a unified framework for zero-shot fraud detection based on Large Language Models. It consists of three core components: (1) Semantic-Enriched Node Encoding. We convert node metadata into descriptive texts and integrate relation-specific neighborhood information. These are fused with original features and encoded using a pretrained relation-aware GNN, yielding node representations enriched with semantic and structural context. (2) Text-Graph Aligner. We introduce learnable query vectors that project graph embeddings into the token space of the LLM, enabling semantic alignment between structured data and natural language representations. (3) In-Context Learning for Zero-Shot Detection. We design a multi-turn prompting strategy that includes self-summary, neighbor summary, and shared behavioral patterns. This guides the LLM to reason over graph-informed text and perform fraud detection without relying on labeled training data.

The main contributions of this paper are as follows:

- We propose FRAUDLLM, a novel zero-shot fraud detection framework that leverages the reasoning power of Large Language Models to analyze graph-structured data without requiring labeled training samples. To our knowledge, this is the first work applying LLMs to fraud detection.
- We introduce a text-graph alignment mechanism using learnable query vectors to bridge structured graph embeddings and LLMs' token space, and further design an in-context prompting strategy that enables LLMs to reason over graph-informed texts and perform zero-shot fraud detection without relying on labeled neighbor data.
- Extensive experiments on two real-world datasets show that FRAUDLLM consistently outperforms competitive baselines in zero-shot settings, demonstrating strong performance in label-scarce scenarios.

2 Preliminaries

Metadata-based Fraud Graph Construction: To construct text-graph data pairs, we first extract the metadata for each node $v \in V$, The metadata includes behavioral details of entities. For instance, in financial systems, it covers aspects like the number of transactions and comprehensive transaction records for fraudulent accounts. On e-commerce platforms, it encompasses timestamps, ratings, and the specific content of reviews for fake reviews.

These relationships, features, and associated information are modeled as a multi-relational fraud graph $G = (\mathcal{V}, \mathcal{E}, \mathcal{X}, \mathcal{M})$. It consists of a set of nodes $\mathcal{V} = \{v, v_2, \ldots, v_N\}(N = |\mathcal{V}|)$ representing N entities, a set of R adjacency matrices $\mathcal{E} = \{A_1, A_2, \ldots, A_R\}(R = |\mathcal{E}|)$ corresponding to types of relationships, a set of raw feature vectors $\mathcal{X} = \{x_1, x_2, \ldots, x_N\}$.and a set of raw metadata $\mathcal{M} = \{m_1, m_2, \ldots, m_N\}$. If $A_r[u, v] = 1$, it indicates that there exists a relationship of type r between entities u and v. Each node $v \in V$ is associated with a d-dimensional raw feature vector $x_v \in \mathbb{R}^d$.

Zero-shot Fraud Detection: Zero-shot fraud detection aims to identify fraudulent nodes in graph G without relying on labeled data. Instead of learning discriminative representations via supervised training, this task leverages node features X, relational structures E, and neighborhood information, guided by a pre-trained Large Language Model (LLM). Contextual embeddings and cue inputs are generated from the graph structure, and anomaly decisions are directly produced by the LLM, enabling detection without task-specific fine-tuning.

3 Method

In this section, we present the proposed framework FRAUDLLM in detail, whose architecture is illustrated in Fig. 2. The framework consists of three core components: Semantic-Enriched Node Encoding, Text-Graph Aligner, and In-Context Learning for Zero-Shot Detection. First, in Semantic-Enriched Node Encoding, node metadata is converted into natural language descriptions using a pre-trained Large Language Model (LLM). These descriptions are then fused with original node features and enriched with relation-specific neighborhood information. The combined inputs are encoded using a pretrained relation-aware GNN, resulting in node representations that capture both semantic and structural contexts. In Text-Graph Aligner, we introduce learnable query vectors that map the graph-based node embeddings into the token space of the LLM, enabling effective semantic alignment between structured representations and natural language inputs. Finally, in In-Context Learning for Zero-Shot Detection, we design a multi-turn prompting strategy that follows a "GenerateâĂŞSummarizeâĂŞInfer" paradigm, incorporating self-description, neighborhood attributes, and shared behavioral patterns. This setup enables the LLM to reason over graph-informed textual data and perform fraud detection without the need for labeled training examples or task-specific fine-tuning.

3.1 Semantic-Enriched Node Encoding

Existing graph-structured data often lacks rich semantic descriptions and primarily provides pre-processed feature vectors. To bridge this gap and enable large language models (LLMs) to effectively interpret graph-based inputs, we construct text-graph pairs that facilitate subsequent cross-modal alignment. In heterogeneous (multi-relational) graphs, this requires capturing both structural dependencies and relation-specific semantics. To achieve this, we introduce

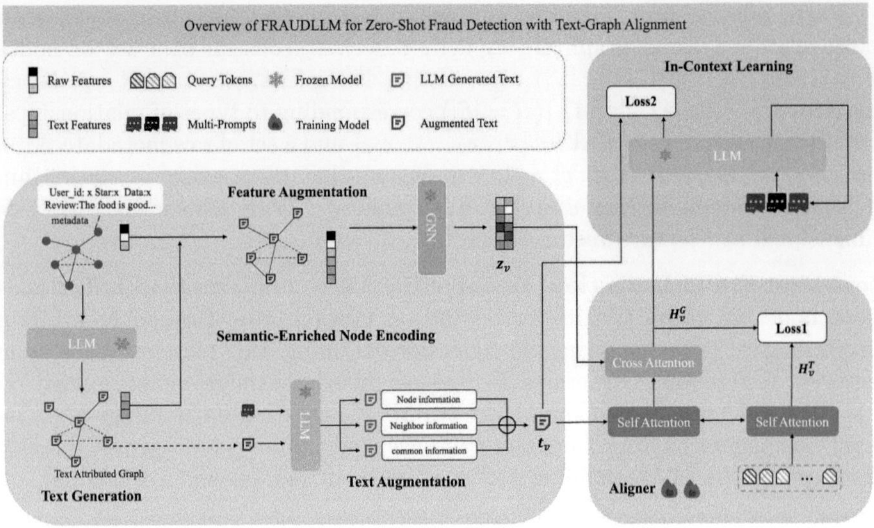

Fig. 2. The proposed FRAUDLLM framework

Semantic-Enriched Node Encoding, which consists of three components: LLM-based textual context generation, feature enrichment via textual integration, and relation-aware neighborhood text augmentation.

LLM-based Textual Context Generation. Given the metadata m_v of any node $v \in V$, we leverage the powerful generative capabilities of large language models (LLMs) to generate natural language descriptions that summarize key information from the node's metadata. This process transforms the original graph into a text-attributed graph, where textual encoders are typically implemented using bag-of-words representations or word embedding models.

$$t_v = \text{LLM}(m_v), \tag{1}$$

$$x_v^{\text{text}} = \text{Encoder}(t_v). \tag{2}$$

Feature Enrichment. After extracting textual attributes, we construct text-graph pairs to facilitate cross-modal alignment, enabling large language models (LLMs) to jointly capture graph structure and node-level semantic information. However, the original node features typically encode only static user attributes and fail to reflect behavioral patterns and contextual interactions—key factors for effective fraud detection. To overcome this limitation, we integrate the generated textual descriptions with the original feature vectors, resulting in enriched node embeddings that encompass a more comprehensive semantic and contextual representation.

$$x_v^{\text{enh}} = \text{MLP}([x_v \parallel x_v^{\text{text}}]), \tag{3}$$

where || denotes the concatenation operation. To further capture structural dependencies in the graph under multi-relational settings and to obtain node embeddings that incorporate structural information, we employ pre-trained relation-aware graph neural networks (e.g., R-GCN or CompGCN) to propagate and aggregate node features. This ensures that the final node embeddings not only encode rich semantic content but also capture the contextual relational patterns embedded in the graph topology.

$$\mathbf{z}_v^{(k)} = \sigma\left(\sum_{r\in R}\sum_{u\in\mathcal{N}_r(v)} \frac{1}{c_{v,r}}\mathbf{W}_r^{(k)}\mathbf{z}_u^{(k-1)} + \mathbf{W}_0^{(k)}\mathbf{z}_v^{(k-1)}\right) \tag{4}$$

Textual Augmentation. To generate high-quality textual descriptions for nodes, we leverage the powerful comprehension and generation capabilities of Large Language Models (LLMs) and design a set of multi-level prompting strategies to guide the model in summarizing node-relevant information from multiple perspectives. Specifically, we construct three core information components for each target node $v \in V$: self-summary $t_v^{(s)}$; neighbor Attributes $t_v^{(n)}$ and shared behavioral patterns $t_v^{(c)}$.

Ultimately, the textual representation of node v is constructed by concatenating the three aforementioned components: $t'_v = \left\{t_v^{(s)},\ t_v^{(n)},\ t_v^{(c)}\right\}$

3.2 Text-Graph Aligner

Large Language Models (LLMs) and Graph Neural Networks (GNNs) operate in fundamentally different representation spaces—LLMs process sequences of discrete tokens, while GNNs output dense continuous embeddings. This modality gap poses a significant challenge when aligning graph-structured data with LLMs for downstream tasks like fraud detection. To address this, we introduce the Text-Graph Aligner, a lightweight yet expressive module inspired by [12], which leverages a set of K learnable query tokens to extract semantically aligned features from node embeddings. This module is trained in two stages:

Stage 1: Cross-Model Pretraining.

To align node embeddings $\mathbf{z}_v$ with textual descriptions t'_v, we encode the text using a pretrained encoder $f_t(\cdot)$ to obtain $\mathbf{h}_t$. A shared self-attention and cross-attention architecture is used to align $\mathbf{z}_v$ with $\mathbf{h}_t$, producing query-guided representations $\mathbf{H}_v^G$ and $\mathbf{H}_v^T$. We train it with three auxiliary objectives:

Text-Graph Contrastive Learning (TGC): Maximize the mutual information between $\mathbf{H}_v^T$ and $\mathbf{H}_v^G$ by measuring their maximum token-level similarity.

$$\mathcal{L}_{\mathrm{g2t}} = -\frac{1}{N}\sum_{i=1}^{N}\log\frac{\exp\left(\mathrm{sim}(H_i^G, H_i^T)/\tau\right)}{\sum_{j=1}^{N}\exp\left(\mathrm{sim}(H_i^G, H_j^T)/\tau\right)} \tag{5}$$

$$\mathcal{L}_{\mathrm{t2g}} = -\frac{1}{N}\sum_{i=1}^{N}\log\frac{\exp\left(\mathrm{sim}(H_i^T, H_i^G)/\tau\right)}{\sum_{j=1}^{N}\exp\left(\mathrm{sim}(H_i^T, H_j^G)/\tau\right)} \tag{6}$$

$$\mathcal{L}_{\mathrm{TGC}} = \mathcal{L}_{\mathrm{g2t}} + \mathcal{L}_{\mathrm{t2g}} \tag{7}$$

Text-Graph Matching (TGM): A binary classifier is applied to the concatenated features $[\mathbf{H}_v^T; \mathbf{H}_v^G]$ to determine whether the text-graph pair is matched or not. $\rho(\mathbf{H}_i^T, \mathbf{H}_i^G)$ denotes TGM's predicted probability that (t'_v, z_v) is matched.

$$\mathcal{L}_{\mathrm{TGM}} = \sum_{i=1}^{N} \left[-\log \rho(\mathbf{H}_i^T, \mathbf{H}_i^G) + \sum_{j \neq i} \log \rho(\mathbf{H}_i^T, \mathbf{H}_j^G) + \sum_{k \neq i} \log \rho(\mathbf{H}_k^T, \mathbf{H}_i^G) \right] \tag{8}$$

Graph Captioning (GCap): We utilize a decoder token [DEC] that replaces [CLS] to autoregressively generate node descriptions from aligned graph embeddings. The generation loss with respect to ground-truth t_v helps enforce fine-grained alignment. $p_\theta(t'_v|\mathbf{H}_v^G)$ denotes the probability that the aligner generates the text t'_v given the graph representation z_v.

$$\mathcal{L}_{\mathrm{GCap}} = -\frac{1}{N} \sum_{i=1}^{N} \log p_\theta(t'_v|\mathbf{H}_v^G) \tag{9}$$

Stage 2: LLM Space Alignment.

After pretraining, the aligned embeddings H_v^G are projected via a linear layer to match the LLM's token embedding space. These aligned tokens serve as soft prompts concatenated with handcrafted instructions for LLM input. The model then generates text conditioned on both the aligned graph representation and textual context, enforcing a final alignment through generation-based loss. $\mathrm{proj}(\cdot)$ denotes the linear projection operation that maps the graph embeddings into the LLM's token embedding space, $p_{\mathrm{LLM}}(\cdot|\cdot)$ represents the conditional probability distribution parameterized by the LLM, t'_i is the target text, and x_i is the corresponding textual context.

$$\mathcal{L}_{\mathrm{Gen}} = -\frac{1}{N} \sum_{i=1}^{N} \log p_{\mathrm{LLM}}(t'_i|\mathrm{proj}(\mathbf{H}_i^G); x_i) \tag{10}$$

3.3 In-Context Learning for Zero-Shot Detection

To enable zero-shot fraud detection, we propose a multi-stage in-context prompting framework that fully leverages the semantic richness and structural context of graph-based data. This framework follows a "GenerateâĂŞSummarizeâĂŞInfer" paradigm, as illustrated in Fig. 3, systematically guiding the large language model through a series of interpretable reasoning steps, all without requiring any task-specific fine-tuning. The prompting strategy incorporates three key components: role definition, task specification, and targeted queries—each carefully crafted to align with the graph topology and relational semantics. This design enables the LLM to comprehend not only the attributes of individual nodes, but

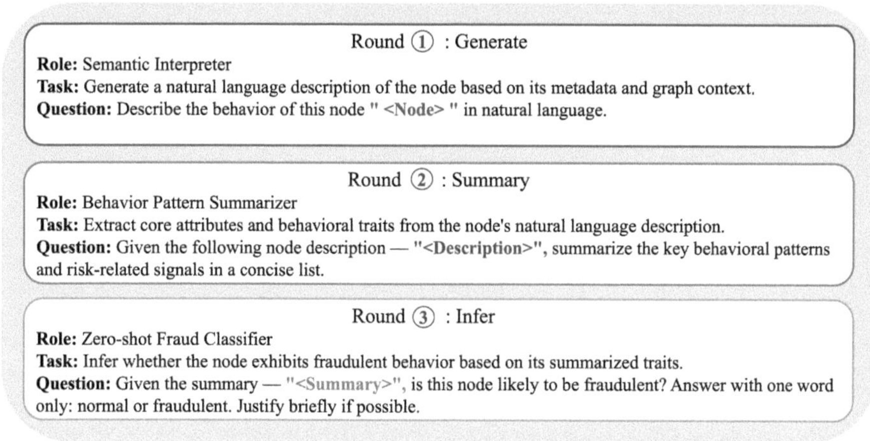

Fig. 3. The prompt of In-Context Learning

also the broader behavioral patterns, local structures, and inter-node dependencies that are essential in identifying complex fraud scenarios.

In the first stage, the LLM generates natural language descriptions for each node by interpreting the semantic and structural cues embedded in the aligned graph representations. These descriptions encapsulate metadata, interaction behaviors, and the roles nodes play within their local subgraphs. Next, the model summarizes this textual input to extract core attributes and neighborhood context, such as frequent transactional patterns or anomalies in user behavior. Finally, using the distilled knowledge and carefully constructed query prompts, the LLM performs inference to determine whether a node exhibits fraudulent behavior. This approach empowers the model to generalize effectively across domains and datasets, offering a scalable and annotation-free solution for fraud detection.

4 Experiments

4.1 Dataset

We conducted experiments on the proposed FRAUDLLM framework using two real-world datasets to evaluate the model's zero-shot fraud detection capability. The statistical details of these datasets are summarized in Table 1.

- YelpChi [17]: This dataset contains both spam (fraudulent) and recommended (legitimate) reviews of hotels and restaurants filtered by Yelp. The nodes in the graph correspond to individual reviews. Since the original dataset lacks node-level metadata, we retrieved the raw data.
- Amazon* [16]: This dataset comprises product reviews from the Amazon Musical Instruments category, with nodes representing users. The original

Table 1. Statistics of Datasets. IR represents the class imbalance ratio.

Dataset	#Nodes(IR)	Relations	#Relations	#Raw Feat
Amazon*	8639 (9.5%)	U-S-U	5599098	25
		U-P-U	294764	
		U-V-U	1386088	
YelpChi	45954 (14.5%)	R-S-R	3402743	32
		R-U-R	49315	
		R-T-R	573616	

data processing method [4] involved randomly selected unlabeled nodes. Due to the randomness of this sampling, metadata for these unlabeled nodes is unavailable, prompting us to optimize the Amazon dataset accordingly.

Table 2. Results on zero-shot fraud detection.

Methods	Amazon*			YelpChi		
	Precision	Recall	F1	Precision	Recall	F1
GCN	0.4531	0.5000	0.4754	0.5160	0.5038	0.3022
GAT	0.4521	0.5000	0.4749	0.4769	0.5018	0.3533
HAN	0.4725	0.4735	0.4469	0.4726	0.5012	0.2773
GraphSAGE	0.5139	0.5306	0.4282	0.5263	0.5035	0.4919
Bert	0.5505	0.6175	0.5394	0.5641	0.5059	0.4793
Roberta	0.6145	0.5243	0.5251	0.4782	0.4992	0.4629
Chatglm-6B	0.5637	0.5015	0.4795	0.5609	0.5016	0.4661
Vicuna-7B-v1.1	0.5717	0.5003	0.4689	0.4389	0.5011	0.4550
Vicuna-7B-v1.5	0.6526	0.5020	0.4798	0.4272	0.4994	0.4605
FRAUDLLM	**0.8456**	**0.7574**	**0.7935**	**0.6177**	**0.6511**	**0.6349**

4.2 Experimental Settings

Baseline. We compare FRAUDLLM with 9 benchmark methods. (1)Representative graph neural network encoders, including GCN [11], GAT [20], HAN [21] and GraphSAGE [6]. (2)Pre-trained Transformer-based language models, such as BERT [3] and RoBERTa [14]. (3)Open-source large language models (LLMs) used as baselines for understanding textual attribute graph data, including ChatGLM2-6B, Vicuna-7B-v1.1, and Vicuna-7B-v1.5.

Evaluation Metrics. We evaluate the effectiveness using the following three metrics: macro-precision, macro-recall, and macro-F1, as these metrics reflect the model's performance on unbalanced data without over-underestimating the minority (fraud) class.

Experimental Environment. All experiments were conducted on a Linux server running Ubuntu 22.04.5, equipped with four NVIDIA A100 GPUs (80 GB VRAM each) and an Intel Xeon Platinum 8360Y CPU @ 2.40 GHz. The proposed FRAUD-LLM framework was implemented using the PyTorch and PyTorch Geometric libraries. The Python and PyTorch versions used were 3.9 and 1.12.1, respectively.

4.3 Overall Performance Evaluation

In the zero-shot setting, GNN models are trained on one dataset and evaluated on another to simulate the zero-sample scenario. For pretrained Transformer-based language models, we calculate similarity between node descriptions and labeled text using prompt-based queries, predicting the class with highest similarity.

We compare FRAUDLLM against nine baseline methods on the Amazon and YelpChi datasets, with the results summarized in Table 2. Overall, FRAUDLLM outperforms all baseline methods across both datasets. Basic GNN models fail to deliver satisfactory fraud detection performance under low-label conditions, primarily due to their strong dependence on labeled data. BERT-based approaches also perform poorly, as they rely solely on similarity calculations and are unable to handle complex zero-shot scenarios effectively. LLM-based solutions such as ChatGLM-6B and Vicuna-7B demonstrate stable performance across different datasets but make predictions based purely on textual information. In contrast, our method retains the structural information of the graph, offering a more comprehensive solution for zero-shot graph fraud detection.

Table 3. The time and space efficiency of the training and inference stages.

Components	dataset	Time(h)	Parameters	GPU Occupy(M)
Text Augment	Amazon*	17.4	-	15520
	Yelpchi	58	-	13738
Pretrain Stage1	Amazon*	0.84	180,935,998	46498
	Yelpchi	4.1	180,935,998	45542
Pretrain Stage2	Amazon*	2	182,936,320	62134
	Yelpchi	9.5	182,936,320	66606
Inference	Amazon*	11.9	-	14878
	Yelpchi	14.6	–	14410

Table 3 summarizes the time and GPU consumption across different stages of our framework on Amazon* and YelpChi. Text augmentation is the most time-consuming, especially on YelpChi due to large-scale text generation. Pre-training Stage 1 is lightweight, while Stage 2 slightly increases GPU usage due to joint optimization. Inference remains efficient with low memory usage. Overall, the framework achieves a good balance between performance and scalability, supporting practical deployment in real-world fraud detection tasks.

4.4 Ablation Study

We conduct an ablation study to evaluate the individual contributions of each submodule in the proposed FRAUDLLM framework. As shown in Table 4, we make the following observations: the Feature Augmentation (FA) module significantly enriches the semantic expressiveness of node representations by integrating raw node features with LLM-generated textual descriptions, resulting in more informative and discriminative embeddings. The Textual Augmentation (TA) module helps the LLM better capture contextual semantics, including behavioral patterns and structural signals from neighboring nodes, which improves fraud detection performance. Moreover, the In-Context Learning (ICL) module, implemented via a multi-turn prompting strategy, greatly enhances the model's reasoning ability under zero-shot settings. Its "GenerateâĂŞSummarizeâĂŞInfer" workflow effectively uncovers latent fraud patterns in the graph, maintaining strong performance even without labeled data.

Table 4. Ablation Results.

Model	Macro-F1	
	Amazon*	YelpChi
w/o FA	0.7339	0.6121
w/o TA	0.6924	0.6086
w/o ICL	0.6218	0.5617
FRAUDLLM	**0.7935**	**0.6349**

In addition, we evaluate FRAUDLLM using different LLM backbones on the Amazon and YelpChi datasets. As shown in Fig. 4, we compare both inference time and Macro-F1 scores across several open-source models, including ChatGLM2-6B, Vicuna-7B-v1.1, Vicuna-7B-v1.3, and Vicuna-7B-v1.5. Among them, Vicuna-7B-v1.5 achieves the best overall performance while offering the fastest inference speed. Balancing accuracy and efficiency, we select Vicuna-7B-v1.5 as the default backbone for FRAUDLLM.

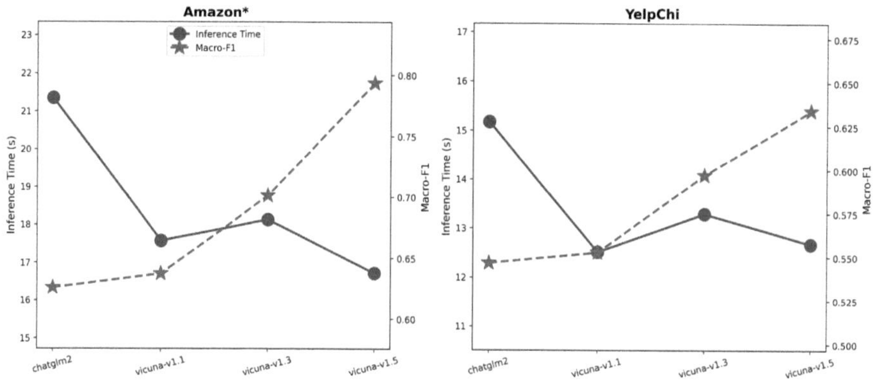

Fig. 4. Performance of different LLM backbones

5 Conclusion

In this paper, we propose FRAUDLLM, the first unified framework to tackle zero-shot fraud detection by integrating Large Language Models with graph-based representations. It addresses the challenge of detecting fraudulent behaviors without any labeled training data by aligning structured graph semantics with natural language understanding. Our framework introduces semantic-enriched node encoding, a novel text-graph alignment mechanism, and an in-context learning strategy tailored for graph-informed reasoning. Through evaluations on real-world datasets, FRAUDLLM consistently outperforms state-of-the-art baselines in zero-shot settings, demonstrating its effectiveness, flexibility, and potential to advance research in fraud detection without supervision.

Despite its strong performance, FRAUDLLM has several limitations. First, the framework requires high-quality and informative node metadata to generate meaningful textual descriptions, which may not be available in all domains. Second, the text-graph alignment module introduces computational overhead and may present scalability issues when applied to large-scale graphs.

References

1. Chen, L., Peng, J., Liu, Y., Li, J., Xie, F., Zheng, Z.: Phishing scams detection in ethereum transaction network. ACM Trans. Internet Technol. (TOIT) **21**(1), 1–16 (2020)
2. Chen, R., Zhao, T., Jaiswal, A., Shah, N., Wang, Z.: Llaga: large language and graph assistant. arXiv preprint arXiv:2402.08170 (2024)
3. Devlin, J., Chang, M.W., Lee, K., Toutanova, K.: Bert: pre-training of deep bidirectional transformers for language understanding. In: Proceedings of the 2019 conference of the North American Chapter of the Association for Computational Linguistics: Human Language Technologies, vol. 1 (long and short papers), pp. 4171–4186 (2019)

4. Dou, Y., Liu, Z., Sun, L., Deng, Y., Peng, H., Yu, P.S.: Enhancing graph neural network-based fraud detectors against camouflaged fraudsters. In: Proceedings of the 29th ACM International Conference on Information & Knowledge Management, pp. 315–324 (2020)
5. Gao, Y., Wang, X., He, X., Liu, Z., Feng, H., Zhang, Y.: Addressing heterophily in graph anomaly detection: a perspective of graph spectrum. In: Proceedings of the ACM Web Conference 2023, pp. 1528–1538 (2023)
6. Hamilton, W., Ying, Z., Leskovec, J.: Inductive representation learning on large graphs. Adv. Neural Inf. Process. Syst. **30** (2017)
7. Hooi, B., Song, H.A., Beutel, A., Shah, N., Shin, K., Faloutsos, C.: Fraudar: bounding graph fraud in the face of camouflage. In: Proceedings of the 22nd ACM SIGKDD International Conference on Knowledge Discovery and Data Mining, pp. 895–904 (2016)
8. Hu, B., et al.: Loan default analysis with multiplex graph learning. In: Proceedings of the 29th ACM International Conference On Information & Knowledge Management, pp. 2525–2532 (2020)
9. Hyun, W., Lee, I., Suh, B.: Lex-GNN: label-exploring graph neural network for accurate fraud detection. In: Proceedings of the 33rd ACM International Conference on Information and Knowledge Management, pp. 3802–3806 (2024)
10. Hyun, W., Lee, J., Suh, B.: Anti-money laundering in cryptocurrency via multi-relational graph neural network. In: Pacific-Asia Conference on Knowledge Discovery and Data Mining, pp. 118–130. Springer (2023)
11. Kipf, T.N., Welling, M.: Semi-supervised classification with graph convolutional networks. arXiv preprint arXiv:1609.02907 (2016)
12. Li, J., Li, D., Savarese, S., Hoi, S.: Blip-2: bootstrapping language-image pre-training with frozen image encoders and large language models. In: International Conference On Machine Learning, pp. 19730–19742. PMLR (2023)
13. Liu, C., et al.: Fraud transactions detection via behavior tree with local intention calibration. In: Proceedings of the 26th ACM SIGKDD International Conference on Knowledge Discovery & Data Mining, pp. 3035–3043 (2020)
14. Liu, Y., et al.: Roberta: a robustly optimized bert pretraining approach. arXiv preprint arXiv:1907.11692 (2019)
15. Liu, Z., Chen, C., Li, L., Zhou, J., Li, X., Song, L., Qi, Y.: Geniepath: graph neural networks with adaptive receptive paths. In: Proceedings of the AAAI Conference On Artificial Intelligence. vol. 33, pp. 4424–4431 (2019)
16. McAuley, J.J., Leskovec, J.: From amateurs to connoisseurs: modeling the evolution of user expertise through online reviews. In: Proceedings of the 22nd international conference on World Wide Web, pp. 897–908 (2013)
17. Rayana, S., Akoglu, L.: Collective opinion spam detection: bridging review networks and metadata. In: Proceedings of the 21th ACM sigkdd International Conference on Knowledge Discovery and Data Mining, pp. 985–994 (2015)
18. Shi, F., Cao, Y., Shang, Y., Zhou, Y., Zhou, C., Wu, J.: H2-fdetector: a GNN-based fraud detector with homophilic and heterophilic connections. In: Proceedings of the ACM Web Conference 2022, pp. 1486–1494 (2022)
19. Tang, J., et al.: Graphgpt: graph instruction tuning for large language models. In: Proceedings of the 47th International ACM SIGIR Conference on Research and Development in Information Retrieval, pp. 491–500 (2024)
20. Veličković, P., Cucurull, G., Casanova, A., Romero, A., Lio, P., Bengio, Y.: Graph attention networks. arXiv preprint arXiv:1710.10903 (2017)
21. Wang, X., et al.: Heterogeneous graph attention network. In: The World Wide Web Conference, pp. 2022–2032 (2019)

22. Wang, Y., et al.: Label information enhanced fraud detection against low homophily in graphs. In: Proceedings of the ACM Web Conference 2023, pp. 406–416 (2023)
23. Wu, B., Yao, X., Zhang, B., Chao, K.M., Li, Y.: Splitgnn: spectral graph neural network for fraud detection against heterophily. In: Proceedings of the 32nd ACM International Conference on Information and Knowledge Management, pp. 2737–2746 (2023)
24. Xiang, S., et al.: Semi-supervised credit card fraud detection via attribute-driven graph representation. In: Proceedings of the AAAI Conference on Artificial Intelligence. vol. 37, pp. 14557–14565 (2023)
25. Xiang, S., et al.: Semi-supervised credit card fraud detection via attribute-driven graph representation. In: Proceedings of the AAAI Conference on Artificial Intelligence. vol. 37, pp. 14557–14565 (2023)
26. Yuan, D., et al.: Detecting fake accounts in online social networks at the time of registrations. In: Proceedings of the 2019 ACM SIGSAC Conference on Computer and Communications Security, pp. 1423–1438 (2019)
27. Zhang, G., Li, Z., Huang, J., Wu, J., Zhou, C., Yang, J., Gao, J.: Efraudcom: an e-commerce fraud detection system via competitive graph neural networks. ACM Trans. Inf. Syst. (TOIS) **40**(3), 1–29 (2022)
28. Zhuo, W., Liu, Z., Hooi, B., He, B., Tan, G., Fathony, R., Chen, J.: Partitioning message passing for graph fraud detection. arXiv preprint arXiv:2412.00020 (2024)

FADE: Progressive Unlearning for Language Models via Adversarial Disruption and Editing

Yang Chen and Zhiwen Tang(✉)

School of Information Science and Engineering, Yunnan University, Kunming, China
chenyang3@stu.ynu.edu.cn, zhiwen.tang@ynu.edu.cn

Abstract. As large language models (LLMs) are increasingly deployed in real-world systems, the ability to selectively remove specific training data, known as machine unlearning, has become essential for privacy protection and compliance. Existing unlearning methods often fall short in this setting: gradient-based approaches risk destabilizing generation, preference-based methods struggle with incomplete forgetting, and parameter-space editing lacks behavioral control. To address these limitations, we propose Forgetting through Adversarial Disruption and Editing (FADE), a progressive framework that decomposes unlearning into three stages. FADE first introduces distributional noise to weaken memorization, then redirects output probabilities away from forgotten targets, at last FADE recovers performance on unaffected data. Experiments on the MUSE benchmark demonstrate that FADE achieves strong forgetting and privacy protection without compromising utility, outperforming prior methods. These results highlight the importance of staged, behavior-level interventions for reliable and controllable unlearning in LLMs.

Keywords: Machine Unlearning · Controllable Forgetting · Large Language Models

1 Introduction

Large language models have demonstrated remarkable generalization capabilities across a wide range of language understanding and generation tasks. However, their ability to memorize specific training data raises significant concerns regarding privacy [1,6], security, and compliance [8]. In this context, the task of machine unlearning [12,17], which aims at removing the influence of a designated subset of training data from a deployed model, has received increasing attention. Compared to unlearning in classification models [5], unlearning in large language models poses unique challenges due to their autoregressive structure, distributed representations, and open-ended output space. An effective unlearning algorithm should suppress the model's ability to generate responses related to a given forget set, while maintaining utility and stability on the remaining data [3] (Fig. 1).

Z. Li et al. (Eds.): CCIR 2025, LNCS 16369, pp. 90–102, 2026.
https://doi.org/10.1007/978-981-95-5637-3_7

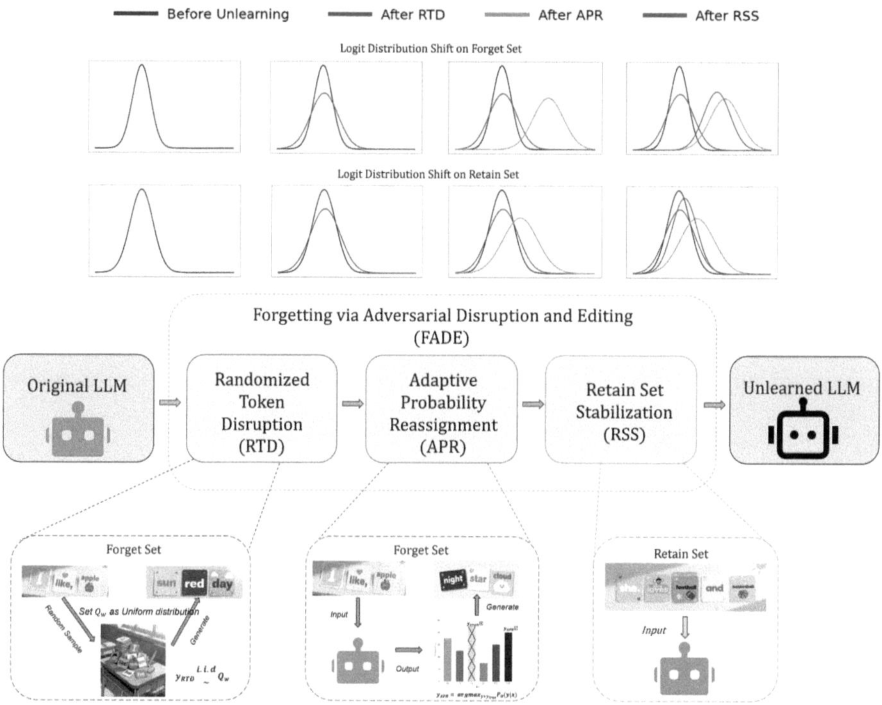

Fig. 1. Overview of FADE.

Existing methods for unlearning in language models can be roughly categorized into two classes. The first class modifies the model's behavior through optimization-based interventions on the output distribution. Representative methods in this category include gradient ascent [5,9], which increases the loss on the forget set to discourage correct generations, and negative preference optimization [18], which reframes forgetting as a pairwise ranking problem between retained and forgotten outputs. While effective in certain settings, these approaches tend to suffer from several limitations. Gradient ascent often causes unstable updates and undesired changes in the generation space. Negative preference optimization, despite its stability improvements, introduces optimization bias due to its reliance on a frozen reference model. More fundamentally, both methods lack mechanisms to redirect the model's outputs toward concrete, controllable alternatives, resulting in limited expressivity and poor consistency across samples.

A second line of work treats unlearning as a representation-level transformation in the model's parameter space. Task vector [7] methods attempt to isolate the influence of the forget set by subtracting the difference between fine-tuned and base model weights [2,10]. Similarly, hyperplane partitioning methods [4] aim to separate retained and forgotten information by constructing orthogonal subspaces in feature space. These approaches are theoretically appealing, but face practical challenges. They typically assume clean task boundaries and rely on linearity in high-dimensional representations, assumptions that rarely hold in real-world generative models. Moreover, they offer limited control over generation behavior, and lack semantic alignment with the model's output structure.

In this work, we present a progressive unlearning framework that addresses the limitations of both output-level and parameter-level methods. Our approach, called FADE, consists of three stages. The first stage applies randomized token disruption by training the model on uniformly generated sequences for the forget set, which reduces confidence in previously learned responses. The second stage, adaptive probability reassignment, constructs pseudo-targets using the model's own output distribution, replacing ground-truth tokens with high-probability alternatives that are semantically close but incorrect. The third stage, retain set stabilization, fine-tunes the model on a separate retain set to restore performance and reduce side effects. This design enables FADE to suppress, redirect, and recover in a controlled and modular manner.

We evaluate the proposed method on the MUSE benchmark [15], a multi-dimensional evaluation framework that assesses unlearning methods in terms of forgetting, retention, generalization, transfer, calibration, and side effects. Experiments across multiple model sizes and datasets show that FADE achieves strong unlearning performance while maintaining competitive retention quality, demonstrating its effectiveness and robustness.

2 Related Work

Machine unlearning for large language models (LLMs) aims to remove specific knowledge without full retraining, providing a practical response to privacy and compliance demands. Existing approaches include gradient-based, preference-based, task vector, and weight-space partitioning methods. Each targets different aspects of the unlearning problem, but often struggles to balance forgetting, retention, and stability.

Gradient-Based Methods. Gradient Ascent (GA) maximizes the loss $\ell(y|x)$ on D_{FG} to suppress specific outputs, but it often degrades D_{RT} performance. Gradient Difference (GD) [11] balances this by minimizing loss on D_{RT} alongside maximizing it on D_{FG}, yet both suffer from unstable optimization and shared representation disruption. Our framework avoids gradient ascent, using input-space disruption and output probability reassignment for precise, stable forgetting.

Preference Optimization Techniques. Some methods regard the LLM unlearning task as a preference optimization problem [13,16]. Negative Preference Optimization (NPO), inspired by Direct Preference Optimization (DPO) [14], penalizes D_{FG} outputs as negative samples, reducing preference but retaining semantic associations. Our approach synthesizes contextually plausible pseudo-tokens via randomized disruption and adaptive reassignment, enhancing privacy.

Task Vector Methods. Task Vector methods compute a weight difference to remove D_{FG}-specific knowledge, assuming linear separability, which may fail for complex LLMs, leading to incomplete forgetting or D_{RT} degradation. Our framework manipulates input and output distributions with greater flexibility.

Weight-space Hyperplane Partitioning (WHP). WHP partitions the weight space to isolate D_{FG} parameters, but its complex optimization struggles with scalability in large LLMs. Our method uses a multi-stage pipeline in input and output spaces for efficient forgetting.

FADE addresses these limitations through staged interventions in the input and output space. RTD weakens memory traces by random disruption, APR reassigns output probabilities away from ground-truth tokens, and RSS restores utility on the retain set. This decoupled structure avoids instability from gradient-based updates, provides contextual output control beyond preference rejection, and maintains flexibility without relying on strict parameter assumptions.

3 Forgetting via Adversarial Disruption and Editing

3.1 Problem Formulation and Framework Overview

The unlearning task aim to selectively *forget* certain pieces of information without retraining the model from scratch. The objective is to remove a model's dependence on specific samples while maintaining its performance on all other data. Formally, let f_θ denote a pre-trained LLM with parameters θ. We define two disjoint datasets: the *forget set* $\mathcal{D}_{\text{FG}}$, containing samples whose influence should be erased from the model, and the *retain set* $\mathcal{D}_{\text{RT}}$, containing samples whose knowledge should be preserved. The goal is to obtain a new model $f_{\theta'}$ such that the outputs on $\mathcal{D}_{\text{FG}}$ are no longer aligned with the original ground-truth answers, while preserving the original behavior on $\mathcal{D}_{\text{RT}}$.

We introduce a progressive multi-stage unlearning framework, Forgetting through Adversarial Disruption and Editing *(FADE)* to balance forgetting effectiveness and retention stability. FADE operates in a coarse-to-fine manner, starting with broad disruption, then applying targeted editing, and finally restoring desired behaviors. The first stage, *Randomized Token Disruption (RTD)*, injects noise into the model by replacing ground-truth answers in $\mathcal{D}_{\text{FG}}$ with fully random sequences. This destabilizes the model's confidence and weakens its reliance on the original outputs. The second stage, *Adaptive Probability Reassignment (APR)*, guides the model away from residual memory traces by constructing pseudo-labels from high-probability but incorrect tokens, based on the model's own predictions. This allows fine-grained editing of the model's output distribution. The final stage, *Retain Set Stabilization (RSS)*, performs continual training on $\mathcal{D}_{\text{RT}}$ to restore and preserve useful knowledge that may have been disturbed during the unlearning process.

In the following sections, we detail the technical formulation and implementation of each stage. For clarity, we denote model parameters at different stages using semantic subscripts: θ_{init} for the original model, θ_{rtd} after randomized token disruption, θ_{apr} after adaptive probability reassignment, and θ_{final} after retain set stabilization. The complete algorithm of FADE is shown in Algorithm 1.

Algorithm 1. Forgetting via Adversarial Disruption and Editing (FADE)

Input: Model f_θ with parameters θ, forget set D_{FG}, retain set D_{RT}, vocabulary $\mathcal{W}$, hyperparameters (T_{RTD}, T_{APR}, T_{RSS})
Output: Updated model $f_{\theta'}$ with unlearned D_{FG} and preserved D_{RT}
Initialize $D_{\text{RTD}} \leftarrow \emptyset$ ▷ Stage 1: Randomized Token Disruption (RTD)
Set Q_w as a Uniform distribution.
for each $(x, y_t) \in D_{\text{FG}}$ **do**
  for $i = 1$ to $length(y_t)$ **do**
    $\tilde{y}_t^{\text{rtd}} \overset{\text{i.i.d.}}{\sim} Q_{\text{W}}$
  end for
  $\tilde{y}^{\text{rtd}} \leftarrow (\tilde{y}_1^{\text{rtd}}, \ldots, \tilde{y}_I^{\text{rtd}})$
  $D_{\text{RTD}} \leftarrow D_{\text{RTD}} \cup (x, \tilde{y}^{\text{rtd}})$
end for
for $t = 1$ to T_{RTD} **do**
  $\theta \leftarrow \text{FineTune}(f_\theta, D_{\text{RTD}})$
end for
Initialize $D_{\text{APR}} \leftarrow \emptyset$ ▷ Stage 2: Adaptive Probability Reassignment (APR)
for each $(x, y_t) \in D_{\text{FG}}$ **do**
  $P_\theta(y|x) \leftarrow f_\theta(x)$
  for $i = 1$ to $length(y_t)$ **do**
    $\tilde{y}_i^{\text{apr}} \leftarrow \arg\max_{w \in \mathcal{W} \setminus \{y_t\}} P_\theta(y_i|x)$
  end for
  $\tilde{y}^{\text{apr}} \leftarrow (\tilde{y}_1^{\text{apr}}, \ldots, \tilde{y}_I^{\text{apr}})$
  $D_{\text{APR}} \leftarrow D_{\text{APR}} \cup (x, \tilde{y}^{\text{apr}})$
end for
for $t = 1$ to T_{APR} **do**
  $\theta \leftarrow \text{FineTune}(f_\theta, D_{\text{APR}})$
end for
for $t = 1$ to T_{RSS} **do** ▷ Stage 3: Retain Set Stabilization (RSS)
  $\theta \leftarrow \text{FineTune}(f_\theta, D_{\text{RT}})$
end for
return $f_{\theta'}$

3.2 Randomized Token Disruption

The first stage of FADE, randomized token disruption (RTD), is designed to induce coarse-grained perturbations in the model's predictive behavior on the forget set $\mathcal{D}_{\text{FG}}$. The core intuition is to reduce the model's confidence in its original output patterns by introducing supervision signals that are syntactically well-formed but semantically unaligned with the input. For each input $x \in \mathcal{D}_{\text{FG}}$, the associated target is replaced with a sequence of tokens sampled uniformly from the vocabulary space. This breaks the alignment between input semantics and target structure, thereby diminishing the model's learned output tendencies without directly reinforcing any alternative.

Formally, let $\mathcal{W}$ denote the vocabulary, and let Q_{W} be the uniform distribution over $\mathcal{W}$. For each sample $(x, y) \in \mathcal{D}_{\mathrm{FG}}$ with target length $T = |y|$, we construct a perturbed pair $(x, \tilde{y}^{\mathrm{rtd}})$, where $\tilde{y}^{\mathrm{rtd}} = (\tilde{y}_1^{\mathrm{rtd}}, \ldots, \tilde{y}_T^{\mathrm{rtd}})$ and each $\tilde{y}_t^{\mathrm{rtd}} \overset{\text{i.i.d.}}{\sim} Q_{\mathrm{W}}$. The model is then fine-tuned to minimize the loss:

$$\theta_{\mathrm{rtd}} = \mathcal{L}_{\mathrm{RTD}}(\theta) = -\sum_{(x,y)\in\mathcal{D}_{\mathrm{FG}}} \log P_\theta(\tilde{y}^{\mathrm{rtd}}|x), \tag{1}$$

where θ_{rtd} denotes the updated model parameters. This procedure induces a shift in the output distribution $P_{\theta_{\mathrm{rtd}}}(y|x)$ away from the original high-probability regions, ideally approaching a flattened, low-confidence form. However, since the sampled targets are entirely random, RTD introduces non-targeted noise that may leave residual output bias toward original tokens, especially if they are structurally frequent or contextually salient. This limitation motivates the second stage, adaptive probability reassignment (APR), which selectively reassigns output probability mass to confounding yet plausible alternatives, enabling precise and model-aware behavioral rewriting.

3.3 Adaptive Probability Reassignment

The second stage of FADE, adaptive probability reassignment (APR), addresses the need for fine-grained control over the model's output behavior on the forget set $\mathcal{D}_{\mathrm{FG}}$. While RTD weakens the model's confidence through input-agnostic noise, it provides no guidance on where the probability mass should be redistributed. APR instead leverages the model's own output distribution to identify plausible yet incorrect alternatives to the ground-truth answers. These alternatives are then used as pseudo-labels to redirect the model's predictions away from the original targets. By anchoring this redirection in the model's own prediction space, APR enables a more structured and linguistically coherent transformation of the output behavior, allowing the model to unlearn by re-preference rather than by random suppression.

Concretely, given an input $x \in \mathcal{D}_{\mathrm{FG}}$, we compute the model's output distribution $P_{\theta_{\mathrm{rtd}}}(y|x)$ and extract a candidate sequence $\tilde{y}^{\mathrm{apr}} = (\tilde{y}_1^{\mathrm{apr}}, \ldots, \tilde{y}_T^{\mathrm{apr}})$ such that each token $\tilde{y}_t^{\mathrm{apr}}$ is chosen as the highest-probability token under $P_{\theta_{rtd}}$ excluding the ground-truth token y_t, i.e.,

$$\tilde{y}_t^{\mathrm{apr}} = \arg\max_{w\in\mathcal{W}\setminus\{y_t\}} P_{\theta_{\mathrm{rtd}}}(w \mid x, y_{<t}). \tag{2}$$

The resulting pseudo-target sequence $\tilde{y}$ is then used to fine-tune the model by minimizing the following loss:

$$\theta_{\mathrm{apr}} = \arg\min_\theta \mathcal{L}_{\mathrm{APR}}(\theta) = -\sum_{(x,y)\in\mathcal{D}_{\mathrm{FG}}} \log P_\theta(\tilde{y}|x) \tag{3}$$

where θ_{apr} denotes the updated parameters. Unlike RTD, APR ensures that the corrupted supervision remains linguistically well-formed and lies close to the model's natural output space. This minimizes training instability while ensuring that probability mass is actively moved away from the true targets, thus refining the forgetting process with distribution-aware supervision.

Critically, APR is only effective when applied after RTD. If APR is applied directly to the pre-trained model, the highest-probability token is often the ground-truth answer, and the next-best alternative typically lies close in semantic space, sometimes differing by only a synonym, paraphrase, or morphological variation. As a result, using these alternatives as pseudo-labels fails to meaningfully shift the model's behavior, since the gradients are weak and the supervision nearly indistinguishable from the original. RTD resolves this by first flattening the output distribution, reducing the dominance of the ground-truth token and making the model more sensitive to adversarial redirection. In this way, APR builds upon the disruption introduced by RTD, pulling the model's output distribution toward non-ground-truth regions. However, both forgetting process may inadvertently alter representations that overlap with the retain set $\mathcal{D}_{\text{RT}}$, especially when the forget and retain domains are semantically entangled. This motivates the final stage of FADE, *Retain Set Stabilization*, which is designed to recover and reinforce the model's retained capabilities.

3.4 Retain Set Stabilization

The final stage of FADE, retain set stabilization (RSS), is designed to safeguard the model's performance on the retain set $\mathcal{D}_{\text{RT}}$, following the disruptive and redirective processes of RTD and APR. While those stages are effective in altering the model's output behavior on the forget set $\mathcal{D}_{\text{FG}}$, they may unintentionally influence parameters that are shared across data domains. This is particularly problematic when the forget and retain sets contain overlapping linguistic patterns, shared entity types, or similar compositional structures. RSS acts as a restoration phase: by re-exposing the model to correctly labeled samples in $\mathcal{D}_{\text{RT}}$, it reinforces desirable outputs, repairs unintended side effects of forgetting, and ensures that the model retains its original capabilities on relevant inputs.

Formally, RSS involves continued supervised fine-tuning on $\mathcal{D}_{\text{RT}}$ using the standard language modeling objective. Given a sample $(x, y) \in \mathcal{D}_{\text{RT}}$, the model is optimized by minimizing the negative log-likelihood:

$$\theta_{\text{final}} = \arg\min_{\theta} \mathcal{L}_{\text{RSS}}(\theta) = - \sum_{(x,y)\in\mathcal{D}_{\text{RT}}} \log P_{\theta}(y|x) \tag{4}$$

where θ_{final} denotes the updated parameters. The objective of this stage is not to overwrite the unlearning effect, but to restore precision in the high-probability output within $\mathcal{D}_{\text{RT}}$, especially for tokens or phrases that may have been indirectly affected during the earlier stages. Since the update is conditioned on ground-truth supervision rather than pseudo-targets or noise, RSS introduces a stabilizing force that aligns the model's behavior with its intended deployment utility, without reintroducing forgotten knowledge. In practice, this stage is lightweight in both compute and optimization complexity, but empirically essential to achieve a balanced trade-off between successful unlearning and retention fidelity.

4 Experiments

4.1 Datasets and Metrics

We evaluate Machine Unlearning Six - way Evaluation (MUSE) to comprehensively assess the effectiveness of FADE. We used the NEWS dataset and BOOKS dataset from MUSE.

NEWS consists of BBC news articles published after August 2023. These articles are randomly partitioned into disjoint forget, retain, and holdout sets. BOOKS is constructed from the original Harry Potter book series and the Harry Potter FanWiki. The forget set contains passages from the original books, while the retain set includes auxiliary information from the fan-curated wiki, allowing for a nuanced assessment of utility preservation under semantically entangled content.

We adopt the evaluation metrics defined by the MUSE benchmark, covering six dimensions. (1) **Verbatim Memory** (VerbMem) quantifies the overlap between model generations and ground-truth continuations for prefix inputs from the forget set $\mathcal{D}_{\mathrm{FG}}$, computed as the average ROUGE-L between $f(x_{[:l]})$ and $x_{[l+1:]}$; lower values indicate better unlearning; (2) **Knowledge Memory** (KnowMem) evaluates factual retention by computing ROUGE between $f(q)$ and a for $(q, a) \in \mathcal{D}_{\mathrm{FG}}$; lower scores imply more effective forgetting; (3) **Privacy Leakage** (PrivLeak) measures the relative AUC gap between the unlearned model and a retrained reference in distinguishing $\mathcal{D}_{\mathrm{FG}}$ from a holdout set $\mathcal{D}_{\mathrm{HO}}$; smaller values indicate better privacy protection; (4) **Utility Preservation** (UtilPres) uses the KnowMem score on the retain set $\mathcal{D}_{\mathrm{RT}}$ to assess whether non-targeted knowledge is preserved, higher values are preferred; (5) **Scalability** tracks VerbMem and UtilPres as the size of $\mathcal{D}_{\mathrm{FG}}$ increases; (6) **Sustainability** evaluates the trend of forgetting quality as the number of unlearning iterations grows. Together, these metrics provide a comprehensive evaluation of forgetting effectiveness, retention fidelity, and practical viability.

Similar to MUSE, we employ GA, GA_{GDR}, GA_{KLR}, NPO, NPO_{GDR}, NPO_{KLR}, Task Vectorand WHPas our baselines, which can be identified from the related work for details.

4.2 Backbone and Parameter Settings

Follow the established protocol in [15], for the NEWS dataset, we use the LLaMA-2 7B model, which was released prior to the publication of the corresponding news content, ensuring no overlap during pretraining. For the BOOKS dataset, we employ the ICLM-7B model, which was trained without access to the Harry Potter series. All experiments are conducted with 1 A100 GPUs. We use AdamW optimizer and *cosinelr_scheduler* in all unlearning experiments.

We use 10 unlearning epochs for all experiments and select the best checkpoint as the base model for next stage. The learning rate of 1e-5 is used in RTD, 5e-5 in APR and 1e-6 in RSS. Additionally, the third stage of the ZeRO optimization strategy and BF16 mixed-precision training is utilized.

Table 1. Main Results.

	C1. No Verbatim Mem.	C2. No Knowledge Mem.	C3. No Privacy Leak.	C4. Utiltiy Preserv.
	VerbMem on $\mathcal{D}_{\text{forget}}$ (↓)	KnowMem on $\mathcal{D}_{\text{forget}}$ (↓)	PrivLeak ($\in [-5\%, 5\%]$)	KnowMem on $\mathcal{D}_{\text{retain}}$ (↑)
News				
Target f_{target}	58.4	63.9	−99.8	55.2
Retrain f_{retrain}	**20.8**	**33.1**	**0.0**	**55.0**
GA	**0.0** ↓**100%**	**0.0** ↓**100%**	5.2 over-unlearn	0.0 ↓100%
GA$_{\text{GDR}}$	4.9 ↓76.5%	31.0 ↓6.3%	108.1 over-unlearn	27.3 ↓50.3%
GA$_{\text{KLR}}$	27.4 ↑31.4%	50.2 ↑51.5%	−96.1 under-unlearn	44.8 ↓18.5%
NPO	**0.0** ↓**100%**	**0.0** ↓**100%**	24.4 over-unlearn	0.0 ↓100.0%
NPO$_{\text{GDR}}$	1.2 ↓94.4%	54.6 ↑64.8%	105.8 over-unlearn	40.5 ↓26.3%
NPO$_{\text{KLR}}$	26.9 ↑29.0%	49.0 ↑48.1%	−95.8 under-unlearn	45.4 ↓17.4%
Task Vector	57.2 ↑174.7%	66.2 ↑100.0%	−99.8 under-unlearn	**55.8** ↑**1.5%**
WHP	19.7 ↓5.6%	21.2 ↓35.9%	109.6 under-unlearn	28.3 ↓48.5%
Ours	7.9 ↓62.0%	29.0 ↓12.4%	**0.02 great-unlearn**	36.8 ↓33.1%
Books				
Target f_{target}	99.8	59.4	−57.5	66.9
Retrain f_{retrain}	**14.3**	**28.9**	**0.0**	**74.5**
GA	**0.0** ↓**100%**	**0.0** ↓**100%**	−25.0 under-unlearn	0.0 ↓100%
GA$_{\text{GDR}}$	**0.0** ↓**100%**	**0.0** ↓**100%**	−26.5 under-unlearn	10.7 ↓85.6%
GA$_{\text{KLR}}$	16.0 ↑11.4%	21.9 ↓24.4%	−40.2 under-unlearn	37.2 ↓50.0%
NPO	**0.0** ↓**100%**	**0.0** ↓**100%**	−24.3 under-unlearn	0.0 ↓100%
NPO$_{\text{GDR}}$	**0.0** ↓**100%**	**0.0** ↓**100%**	−30.8 under-unlearn	22.8 ↓69.4%
NPO$_{\text{KLR}}$	17.0 ↑18.2%	25.0 ↓13.4%	−43.5 under-unlearn	44.6 ↓40.1%
Task Vector	99.7 ↑595.0%	52.4 ↑81.2%	−57.5 under-unlearn	**64.7** ↓**13.1%**
WHP	18.0 ↑25.2%	55.7 ↑92.9%	56.5 over-unlearn	63.6 ↓14.6%
Ours	3.6 ↓74.8%	7.3 ↓74.7%	**-23.9 under-unlearn**	57.6 ↓22.7%

The results are highlighted in blue if the unlearning algorithm satisfies the criterion and in orange otherwise.For privacy leakage, large positive values suggest over-unlearn, while large negative values suggest under-unlearn, and appropriate values suggest great-unlearn.

4.3 Main Results

Table 1 and Fig. 2 reports the experiment results. FADE outperforms prior unlearning methods by addressing core limitations in forgetting effectiveness, utility retention, and privacy protection.

First, FADE achieves strong forgetting with minimal compromise to retention. Gradient-based methods such as GAsuppress VerbMem and KnowMem to near zero, but at the cost of severe utility degradation on the retain set $\mathcal{D}_{\mathrm{RT}}$. Similarly, NPOalso exhibits the same issue, where significant compromise to retention occurs while attempting to achieve forgetting. Regularized variants like $\mathsf{GA}_{\mathsf{GDR}}$, $\mathsf{GA}_{\mathsf{KLR}}$, $\mathsf{NPO}_{\mathsf{GDR}}$and $\mathsf{NPO}_{\mathsf{KLR}}$improve utility but introduce forgetting rebounds, reflecting an unresolved trade-off. Among these methods, $\mathsf{NPO}_{\mathsf{KLR}}$demonstrates relatively better results in balancing forgetting performance and utility retention. In contrast, FADE demonstrates the best balance, achieving low forgetting scores while maintaining higher UtilPres, benefiting from the separation of disruption (RTD) and redirection (APR) from utility recovery (RSS).

Second, FADE offers more precise control over forgetting than preference-based and weight-space approaches. Methods like $\mathsf{NPO}_{\mathsf{GDR}}$and $\mathsf{NPO}_{\mathsf{KLR}}$prioritize retention through output-level suppression but fail to eliminate memorized content, as shown by elevated forgetting metrics. Similarly, Task Vector and WHPretain utility but leave forgetting largely unaddressed. FADE avoids this imbalance by directly modifying output behavior through APR, informed by prior destabilization from RTD.

Third, FADE exhibits better privacy performance. While most baselines either under-unlearn or excessively disrupt shared representations, leading to unstable PrivLeak, FADE achieves near-zero PrivLeak on NEWS and consistently outperforms others on BOOKS, showing reliable knowledge removal without overfitting to deletion.

In scalability and sustainability evaluations, FADE performs comparably to baselines but does not show clear advantages. As the size of the forget set or the number of unlearning rounds increases, both forgetting and retention slightly decline. While overall behavior remains stable, further improvements may require adaptive scheduling or more robust retention mechanisms.

(a) Scalability: Utility Preservation vs. Forget Set Size

(b) Sustainability: Utility preservation vs. Unlearning Requests

Fig. 2. Scalability and Sustainability.

4.4 Ablation Studies

We conduct ablation studies to analyze the contributions of RTD, APR, and RSS using the NEWS and BOOKS datasets. The evaluation focuses on four MUSE metrics: VerbMem, KnowMem, PrivLeak, and UtilPres. Results are summarized in Table 2.

Table 2. Ablation results.

	C1. No Verbatim Mem.	C2. No Knowledge Mem.	C3. No Privacy Leak.		C4. Utiltiy Preserv.
	VerbMem on $\mathcal{D}_{\text{forget}}$ (↓)	KnowMem on $\mathcal{D}_{\text{forget}}$ (↓)	PrivLeak ($\in [-5\%, 5\%]$)		KnowMem on $\mathcal{D}_{\text{retain}}$ (↑)
		News			
Target f_{target}	58.4	63.9	−99.8		55.2
Retrain f_{retrain}	**20.8**	**33.1**	**0.0**		**55.0**
Only RTD	13.1 ↓37.0%	32.5 ↓1.8%	57.7	over-unlearn	33.9 ↓38.4%
Only APR	24.6 ↑18.3%	52.9 ↑59.8%	−99.8	under-unlearn	**39.6 ↓28.0%**
RTD + RSS	12.3 ↓40.8%	32.2 ↓2.7%	47.9	over-unlearn	34.6 ↓37.1%
RTD + APR	**7.9 ↓62.0%**	**29.0 ↓12.4%**	**0.02**	**great-unlearn**	36.8 ↓33.1%
RTD + RSS + APR	8.9 ↓57.2%	29.3 ↓11.5%	−14.6	under-unlearn	35.5 ↓35.5%
RTD + APR + RSS	8.0 ↓61.5%	28.9 ↓12.7%	−8.0	under-unlearn	36.2 ↓34.2%
		Books			
Target f_{target}	99.8	59.4	−57.5		66.9
Retrain f_{retrain}	**14.3**	**28.9**	**0.0**		**74.5**
Only RTD	**0.0 ↓100%**	**0.0 ↓100%**	−45.9	under-unlearn	40.9 ↓45.1%
Only APR	8.2 ↓42.3%	26.9 ↓6.9%	−63.8	under-unlearn	47.6 ↓36.1%
RTD + RSS	9.2 ↓35.7%	23.5 ↓18.7%	−30.1	under-unlearn	46.2 ↓38.0%
RTD + APR	**0.0 ↓100%**	0.2 ↓99.3%	−33.9	under-unlearn	54.4 ↓27.0%
RTD + RSS + APR	7.4 ↓48.3%	15.8 ↓45.3%	**−22.3**	**under-unlearn**	54.5 ↓26.8%
RTD + APR + RSS	**0.0 ↓100%**	0.7 ↓97.6%	−32.5	under-unlearn	**56.8 ↓23.8%**

RTD introduces random supervision to suppress memorized outputs. It reduces confidence in the original responses but does not remove them effectively. High PrivLeak and low UtilPres in the RTD-only setting confirm that the model becomes uncertain rather than forgetful.

APR shifts output probability toward incorrect alternatives. Applied alone, it performs inconsistently: on BOOKS, PrivLeak is highly negative, indicating under-unlearning. This shows that APR requires a flattened output distribution to be effective.

Combining RTD and APR leads to substantial improvements across forgetting and privacy metrics. On NEWS, this configuration achieves the best PrivLeak and balanced VerbMem and KnowMem, confirming the complementary roles of disruption and redirection.

RSS improves UtilPres by fine-tuning on the retain set. When applied after RTD or RTD+APR, it recovers utility but may weaken forgetting. For instance, applying RSS after RTD+APR slightly increases KnowMem and decreases

PrivLeak quality on BOOKS, reflecting a trade-off between retention and erasure.

Among all configurations, RTD+APR provides the best balance between privacy, forgetting, and utility. RSS further improves retention when needed. FADE's staged design enables precise control of forgetting behavior while maintaining overall model utility.

The results are highlighted in blue if the unlearning algorithm satisfies the criterion and in orange otherwise. For privacy leakage, large positive values suggest over-unlearn, while large negative values suggest under-unlearn, and appropriate values suggest great-unlearn.

5 Conclusion and Future Work

This work introduces FADE, a staged framework for unlearning in large language models. By separating disruption (RTD), redirection (APR), and recovery (RSS), FADE balances forgetting, privacy, and utility. Experiments on the MUSE benchmark show that FADE outperforms prior methods across forgetting quality, privacy leakage, and retention stability. Its modular design addresses key limitations of gradient-based, preference-based, and weight-space approaches.

Future directions include adaptive stage scheduling, generalization to continual and instruction tuning settings, and alignment with real-world compliance and auditing requirements.

Acknowledgments. This work is supported by Yunnan Fundamental Research Project (202501AT070231) and Open Research Project of the Yunnan University Resilience and Excellence Children's Character Development Platform (K207003250007).

References

1. Carlini, N., Ippolito, D., Jagielski, M., Lee, K., Tramer, F., Zhang, C.: Quantifying memorization across neural language models. In: The Eleventh International Conference on Learning Representations (2022)
2. Chen, J., Yang, D.: Unlearn what you want to forget: Efficient unlearning for llms. arXiv preprint arXiv:2310.20150 (2023)
3. Dang, Q.-V.: Right to be forgotten in the age of machine learning. In: Antipova, T. (ed.) ICADS 2021. AISC, vol. 1352, pp. 403–411. Springer, Cham (2021). https://doi.org/10.1007/978-3-030-71782-7_35
4. Eldan, R., Russinovich, M.: Who's harry potter? approximate unlearning in LLMs. **1**(2), 8 (2023). https://arxiv.org/abs/2310.02238
5. Golatkar, A., Achille, A., Soatto, S.: Eternal sunshine of the spotless net: selective forgetting in deep networks. In: Proceedings of the IEEE/CVF Conference on Computer Vision and Pattern Recognition, pp. 9304–9312 (2020)
6. Huang, J., Shao, H., Chang, K.C.C.: Are large pre-trained language models leaking your personal information? arXiv preprint arXiv:2205.12628 (2022)

7. Ilharco, G., et al.: Editing models with task arithmetic. arXiv preprint arXiv:2212.04089 (2022)
8. Jang, J., et al.: Knowledge unlearning for mitigating privacy risks in language models. arXiv preprint arXiv:2210.01504 (2022)
9. Jia, J., et al.: Model sparsification can simplify machine unlearning. arXiv preprint arXiv:2304.04934 **1**(2), 3 (2023)
10. Kumar, V.B., Gangadharaiah, R., Roth, D.: Privacy adhering machine un-learning in NLP. arXiv preprint arXiv:2212.09573 (2022)
11. Liu, B., Liu, Q., Stone, P.: Continual learning and private unlearning. In: Conference on Lifelong Learning Agents, pp. 243–254. PMLR (2022)
12. Maini, P., Feng, Z., Schwarzschild, A., Lipton, Z.C., Kolter, J.Z.: Tofu: a task of fictitious unlearning for LLMs. arXiv preprint arXiv:2401.06121 (2024)
13. Ouyang, L., et al.: Training language models to follow instructions with human feedback. Adv. Neural. Inf. Process. Syst. **35**, 27730–27744 (2022)
14. Rafailov, R., Sharma, A., Mitchell, E., Manning, C.D., Ermon, S., Finn, C.: Direct preference optimization: your language model is secretly a reward model. Adv. Neural. Inf. Process. Syst. **36**, 53728–53741 (2023)
15. Shi, W., et al.: Muse: Machine unlearning six-way evaluation for language models. arXiv preprint arXiv:2407.06460 (2024)
16. Stiennon, N., et al.: Learning to summarize with human feedback. Adv. Neural. Inf. Process. Syst. **33**, 3008–3021 (2020)
17. Yao, J., et al.: Machine unlearning of pre-trained large language models. arXiv preprint arXiv:2402.15159 (2024)
18. Zhang, R., Lin, L., Bai, Y., Mei, S.: Negative preference optimization: From catastrophic collapse to effective unlearning. arXiv preprint arXiv:2404.05868 (2024)

MMKRF: A Domain-Specific Knowledge Retrieval Framework for RAG Systems in Materials Mechanics

Zhen Hu[1], Qinglong Duan[2], Bing Liu[2], and Yanjie Li[1](✉)

[1] Beijing Forestry University, Beijing 100084, China
{huzhen,liyanjie}@bjfu.edu.cn
[2] Beijing Yi Xin Information Technology Co., Ltd, Beijing 200233, China
{duanqinglong,liubingY}@yxqiche.com

Abstract. Retrieval-Augmented Generation effectively mitigates hallucination issues in model generation by integrating the intrinsic knowledge of large language models with external knowledge bases. The performance of the retriever directly impacts the response quality of RAG systems in knowledge-intensive scenarios. However, existing retrieval algorithms and models predominantly designed for general domains, often exhibiting limited performance in specialized fields. To address this issue, this paper proposes a domain-specific knowledge retrieval framework named MMKRF, which accomplishes retrieval tasks in the field of material mechanics through three stages: recall, multi-path fusion, and re-ranking. Optimization strategies such as explicit knowledge enhancement, domain-specific vocabulary expansion, and domain-adaptive fine-tuning are employed to enhance the algorithms and models involved in the framework. Experimental results demonstrate that MMKRF exhibits excellent domain adaptability: on the material mechanics course knowledge retrieval dataset, MMKRF achieves a notable 5% improvement in accuracy (Acc) compared to baseline frameworks, while Recall@5 and MRR@5 increase by 1.3% and 3.4%, and Recall@10 and MRR@10 improve by 0.7% and 3.4%, respectively. These results underscore the framework's robust recall capabilities and its excellent top-ranking performance, enabling the provision of high-quality retrieval result sets for RAG systems.

Keywords: Knowledge retrieval · Retrieval-augmented generation · Large language model · Domain adaptation optimization

1 Introduction

Despite the remarkable success of Large Language Models (LLMs), they still suffer from inherent limitations. Relying solely on their internal parametric knowledge, LLMs may encounter issues such as outdated information or a lack of domain-specific knowledge, leading to hallucinations [1, 2]. Retrieval-Augmented Generation (RAG) is a technique that integrates information retrieval with text generation [3]. By incorporating external knowledge sources (e.g., document collections, databases, or the internet), RAG systems

Z. Li et al. (Eds.): CCIR 2025, LNCS 16369, pp. 103–118, 2026.
https://doi.org/10.1007/978-981-95-5637-3_8

dynamically retrieve relevant information during generation, thereby expanding model's knowledge coverage and improving output quality without requiring model retraining. This approach is particularly suitable for applications demanding high factual accuracy or domain-specific expertise [4–6]. For instance, in educational Q&A systems, RAG tightly aligns LLMs with curricular knowledge, improving answer accuracy and ensuring responses adhere to disciplinary standards and syllabus requirements.

In RAG systems, the retriever serves as a core component, and its ability to accurately retrieve relevant information based on queries directly impacts the final generation quality [7]. When the retrieved context is insufficiently accurate, it can adversely affect the output of LLMs, exacerbating hallucinations [8, 9]. LLMs struggle to robustly utilize information in long contexts, exhibiting a pronounced positional bias—they perform best when key information is located at the beginning of the context [10]. Therefore, prioritizing the ranking position of relevant information is also important. In knowledge retrieval scenarios, domain-specific knowledge often involves strict terminological systems, conceptual relationships, and logical hierarchies. This necessitates that the retriever transcends mere general semantic relevance calculations and attains a nuanced understanding of domain-specific knowledge, thereby facilitating logical deductions.

However, a single retrieval algorithm struggles to handle complex retrieval scenarios requiring domain-specific knowledge. Typically, a multi-module knowledge retrieval framework is needed, where different algorithms or models collaborate to achieve precise matching between queries and knowledge passages. Existing knowledge retrieval frameworks predominantly designed for general scenarios [11], with limited research on domain adaptability [12]. To address these issues, this paper focuses on knowledge retrieval in the field of materials mechanics as a case study, investigating a lightweight retrieval framework with strong domain adaptability. Our contributions are as follows:

Multi-stage Retrieval Framework for Course Knowledge. We propose a Materials Mechanics Knowledge Retrieval Framework (MMKRF). For each query, MMKRF first employs multiple retrieval methods to rapidly recall relevant knowledge passages, then generates a preliminary candidate set through multi-path retrieval fusion, and finally applies a re-ranking model to enhance the top-ranking accuracy. Our framework provides a standardized retrieval paradigm for course knowledge retrieval.

Transferable Domain Adaptation Optimization Methods. We achieve cost-efficient domain adaptation through incremental optimization of existing models and algorithms. Specifically, we propose two enhancements to the traditional BM25 algorithm: domain-specific vocabulary expansion and explicit knowledge incorporation. For vector retrieval and re-ranking, we employ fine-tuning with improved training techniques, including grouped hybrid negative sampling and prompt-based learning. Our method ology can be easily transferred to other course retrieval tasks and even other specialized domains.

Course Knowledge Retrieval Dataset Construction. Using a combination of data synthesis and manual annotation, we construct the Materials Mechanics Course Knowledge Retrieval (MMCKR) dataset. This work provides a reference for constructing knowledge retrieval datasets in other domains.

2 Related Work

Retrieval Methods. Based on different information encoding approaches, retrieval methods can generally be categorized into sparse and dense types. Sparse retrieval calculates relevance by statistically features [13, 14], offering advantages such as computational efficiency and low hardware requirements. However, its unsupervised nature means retrieval performance is directly constrained by the quality of the original queries and knowledge base, often requiring further optimization of statistical features in specialized domain applications. In contrast, dense retrieval employs neural networks to map queries and documents into a continuous vector space [15–17], measuring textual relevance through vector distance. Such methods are typically trainable, granting them greater flexibility and potential for domain adaptation. Research has shown that fine-tuning can activate domain-specific knowledge acquired during the pretraining phase [18]. Therefore, fine-tuning can further enhance the embedding alignment between queries and relevant texts within a specific domain [19].

Retrieval Augmentation. To improve retrieval accuracy, researchers have proposed various pre-retrieval and post-retrieval augmentation strategies to further enhance the retriever's input and output. Since users often struggle to formulate precise queries directly, pre-retrieval techniques optimize queries through methods such as query expansion (transforming single queries into multiple enriched versions) [20], query rewriting (disambiguating and clarifying intent via semantic parsing) [21], and query routing (dynamically selecting processing pipelines for different retrieval scenarios). Post-retrieval augmentation refines the top-k retrieved passages before passing them to the generator, including re-ranking (combining results from different retrieval methods for robustness) [22] and filtering (removing low-relevance passages to reduce noise) [23], thereby improving synergy between the retriever and generator.

In this paper, we propose MMKRF, a lightweight multi-stage retrieval framework that combines diverse methods and retrieval-augmented strategies, achieving strong performance and domain transferability.

3 Our Framework

MMKRF is a multi-stage retrieval framework comprising recall, fusion, and re-ranking stages, ultimately outputting a refined set of knowledge passages that meet RAG system requirements, as shown in Fig. 1. The framework incorporates domain-adaptive optimizations at each stage, where module-level enhancements collectively improve overall retrieval performance while maintaining excellent cross-domain transferability.

3.1 Recall Stage

The recall stage is responsible for efficiently retrieving query-relevant knowledge passages from external knowledge bases. MMKRF employs both sparse retrieval (BM25_atire [24]) and dense retrieval (BGE-M3-Embedding [17]). For sparse retrieval, which calculates text relevance through term statistics, we propose two optimization strategies to improve term computation accuracy: **domain-specific vocabulary expansion** and **explicit knowledge enhancement**. For dense retrieval, where relevance is measured by cosine similarity between semantic vectors, MMKRF performs **domain-adaptive fine-tuning** on the vector retrieval model to obtain more domain-aligned vector representations.

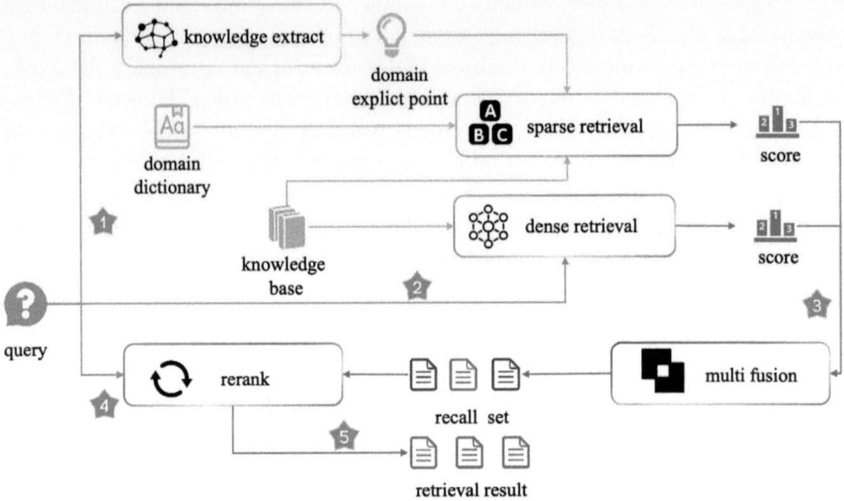

Fig. 1. MMKRF multi-stage retrieval flowchart

Domain-Specific vocabulary Expansion. Text relevance calculation based on statistical learning relies heavily on accurate word segmentation. However, languages like Chinese lack explicit word boundaries, making segmentation particularly challenging. Specialized domains often contain numerous technical terms, while general-purpose segmentation tools trained on generic corpora risk incorrect segmentation of domain-specific word. The atomic splitting of technical terms can compromise their semantic integrity. Domain vocabulary expansion addresses these challenges by defining minimal semantic units to ensure proper term participation in relevance computation. LLMs can automate the construction of domain-specific vocabulary. In MMKRF, we merge the material mechanics vocabulary with the general vocabulary and use the Jieba[1] segmentation tool to construct a new prefix dictionary based on the combined vocabulary, thereby improving the accuracy of domain-specific word segmentation.

Explicit Knowledge Enhancement. Natural language queries often implicitly contain core domain concepts, yet their absence in explicit query terms leads to inaccurate term-based relevance scoring. Explicit knowledge enhancement addresses this by extracting latent knowledge from queries and incorporating these elements as formal query terms, thereby mapping surface-level questions to specialized conceptual spaces. Furthermore, queries may contain non-standard terminology, necessitating normalization

[1] https://github.com/fxsjy/jieba

to canonical terms to ensure lexical homogeneity during computation. Our approach first employs LLMs for explicit knowledge extraction from queries, then combines the extracted knowledge components with the original query to form an enhanced representation. This final query formulation undergoes pairwise relevance computation with knowledge passages.

Domain-Adaptive Fine-Tuning for Dense Model. Domain-adaptive fine-tuning involves further training the base model with a small amount of incremental domain-specific data to adjust the parameter weights in its neural network. This process enables the model to restructure its feature representation space, capturing domain-specific semantic patterns and knowledge associations while improving its ability to disambiguate domain-specific terms and handle long-tail queries with greater robustness. In MMKRF, we perform domain-adaptive fine-tuning on the dense retrieval model using the standard InfoNCE loss:

$$L = -log\frac{\exp(s(q, p^{+})/\tau)}{\sum_{p\in\{p^{+},p^{-}\}}\exp(s(q, p)/\tau)} \tag{1}$$

During training, we employ a **grouped hybrid sampling strategy** (Sect. 6.2) that combines hard negative samples with random negative samples, effectively improving the fine-tuning outcomes.

3.2 Multi-path Fusion Stage

Sparse and dense retrieval methods exhibit fundamental differences in their retrieval dimensions, yet they are not mutually exclusive but rather potentially complementary. For details, see Sect. 6.3. Specifically, BM25-based sparse retrieval demonstrates advantages in exact term matching and local statistical features, while embedding-based dense retrieval excels at semantic understanding and global feature capturing. To compensate for the precision limitations of individual indexing methods, MMKRF integrates both approaches to enhance overall retrieval framework performance.

For dense retrieval, relevance scores s_{dense} are obtained by computing cosine similarity between query and document vectors, naturally bounded within [0, 1]. In contrast, BM25 produces theoretically unbounded scores s_{sparse} ranging $[0, +\infty)$ without predefined limits. To enable effective fusion of these heterogeneous scoring systems, MMKRF applies sigmoid normalization to map BM25 scores into the [0, 1] interval:

$$s_{sparse}^{norm} = sigmoid(s_{sparse}(q, p)) \tag{2}$$

Then, the framework employs **linear weighted fusion (LWF)**, combining relevance scores from both retrieval methods through weighted summation:

$$s_{LWF}(q, p) = \alpha \cdot s_{sparse}^{norm}(q, p) + (1 - \alpha) \cdot s_{dense}(q, p) \tag{3}$$

The fusion factor $\alpha \in (0,1)$ controls the relative weighting of different retrieval methods in the combined results. We set α equal to 0.4, with detailed discussion in Sect. 6.4. The top 10 passages are retained based on the final score s_{LWF} to form the preliminary retrieval candidate set.

3.3 Re-Ranking Stage

The re-ranking stage performs precise ordering by recalculating relevance scores between the query and knowledge passages generated from the fusion stage. MMKRF employs the bge-reranker-v2-minicpm-layerwise model for re-ranking, which is based on LLM. The model computes relevance scores by projecting the hidden states of the last token from each layer onto the vocabulary distribution, using the logit corresponding to 'yes' as the layer-wise relevance score.

Domain-Adaptive Fine-Tuning for the Re-ranking Model. Pre-trained on general corpora, the re-ranking model exhibits limitations when processing domain-specific data. Distributional discrepancies in domain data—including specialized terminology, knowledge structures, and the complexity of user query intent—may lead to biased feature extraction, consequently degrading ranking performance. To address this, MMKRF employs LoRA[25] for efficient fine-tuning, specifically adapting layers 8–40 of the model. The training also utilizes InfoNCE loss. The framework further enhances fine-tuning outcomes through **1) Grouped hybrid sampling. 2) Prompt optimization techniques** (Sect. 6.5). The final implementation selects the optimal layer for re-ranking through comprehensive evaluation of each tuned layer's performance.

4 Dataset

To advance research in knowledge retrieval tasks, we introduce the **Materials Mechanics Course Knowledge Retrieval (MMCKR)** dataset[2]. Each data instance comprises a domain-specific query-knowledge passage pair from materials mechanics with strictly one-to-one relevance mapping.

Data Collection. We manually segment classical textbooks on materials mechanics, organizing knowledge passages along core conceptual frameworks to form the original knowledge set K_{origin}. Each passage encapsulates a complete atomic knowledge unit. Additionally, we compile question sets Q containing domain-specific queries and descriptions aligned with chapter structures.

Train Dataset. The construction of the train dataset is divided into two stages. During the **knowledge passage generation stage**, four advanced LLMs are employed to paraphrase all knowledge passages in K_{origin}. This process generates four expanded sets K_i, where $i \in$ {qwen, ernie, moonshot, spark}. In the **query extraction stage**, knowledge questions and key points are extracted from each knowledge passage and paired with it. The corresponding passage serves as the only relevant passage p^+ for these queries, while other passages in the set are considered irrelevant p^-. This process results in 8,340 query–knowledge passage pairs, forming the training dataset.

Test Dataset. The construction of the test set mainly relies on manual annotation. Each query in Q is matched one-to-one with knowledge passage from K_{origin}. This process is carried out independently by two annotators and is followed by cross-validation. Ultimately, a total of 1,560 query-knowledge passage pairs are constructed through this procedure, forming the test dataset.

[2] https://github.com/hank317/MMCKR-dataset.

5 Experiment

The MMKRF consists of multiple retrieval stages, each employing distinct algorithms and models. Through experiments, we 1) verify the effectiveness of MMKRF's domain adaptability optimization across all modules, and 2) demonstrate the superiority of MMKRF in knowledge retrieval tasks for the course of materials mechanics.

5.1 Experimental Settings

Sparse retrieval uses four BM25 variants[3]: BM25_robertson, BM25_lucene, BM25 +, and BM25_atire. For dense retrieval, we select four state-of-the-art dual-tower models: Tao-8k, text-embedding-3-large, jina-embeddings-v3, and BGE-M3-Embedding, to support long-text encoding. The re-ranking stage employs three advanced interactive models: bge-reranker-v2-m3, bge-reranker-v2-minicpm-layerwise, and bge-reranker-v2.5-gemma2-lightweight. To adapt to the target domain, MMKRF performs full-parameter fine-tuning on the BGE-M3-Embedding ($batch\_size = 16$, $epochs = 2$, $lr = $ 1e-5, $warmup\_ratio = 0.1$, with two sampling groups of 8 samples each). Additionally, LoRA fine-tuning is applied to bge-reranker-v2-minicpm-layerwise, targeting the qkv/o matrices in the attention blocks and the llm_head layer ($rank = 32$, $alpha = 64$, $batch\_size = 16$, $epochs = 1$, $lr = $ 2e-4, with two sampling groups of 8 samples each). The baseline for the experiments follows the same multi-stage retrieval pipeline as MMKRF, but without applying any domain adaptability optimization.

5.2 Metrics

We select three important evaluation metrics: Accuracy (Acc) measures whether the top 1 result retrieved by the model is a relevant knowledge passage; Recall@k assesses whether the relevant knowledge passage is included within the top k retrieved results; and Mean Reciprocal Rank (MRR@k) reflects the model's ability to effectively rank knowledge passages.

5.3 Main Results

Retrieval. As shown in the "retriever" row of Table 1. Domain adaptability improvements enhance term feature accuracy, making sparse retrieval more precise. Without domain fine-tuning, dense retrieval underperforms compared to simple sparse retrieval, indicating that general dense models fail to grasp domain-specific knowledge as effectively as term-based features. After fine-tuning, dense models produce higher-quality vector representations, significantly boosting retrieval performance and surpassing sparse retrieval. This also underscores the limitation of sparse retrieval in adapting to specific domains.

[3] https://github.com/hank317/BM25-series.

Table 1. Experimental results of different retrieval modules on the MMCKR dataset across all retrieval stages, where † indicates that the module has undergone domain adaptation optimization. The best results in each stage are indicated by underlining, and the overall best results across all stages are shown in bold.

Stage	Model	Acc	Recall@k		MRR@k	
			$k = 5$	$k = 10$	$k = 5$	$k = 10$
retriever	BM25_robertson	0.690	0.902	0.947	0.772	0.778
	BM25_lucene	0.707	0.912	0.953	0.786	0.792
	BM25 +	0.703	0.901	0.947	0.779	0.785
	BM25_atire	0.705	0.912	0.953	0.785	0.791
	BM25_atire†	0.747	0.935	0.968	0.822	0.827
	Tao	0.635	0.896	0.943	0.741	0.747
	text-embedding	0.620	0.896	0.951	0.730	0.738
	jina	0.628	0.891	0.942	0.733	0.740
	BGE	0.657	0.909	0.956	0.759	0.766
	BGE†	0.819	0.957	0.976	0.876	0.878
fusion	BM25 with BGE	0.756	0.942	0.974	0.832	0.837
	BM25† with BGE†	0.845	**0.968**	0.981	0.897	0.899
reranker	m3	0.731	0.906	0.953	0.800	0.806
	gemma2-lightweight	0.769	0.942	0.974	0.841	0.845
	minicpm-layerwise	0.805	0.944	0.972	0.863	0.867
	minicpm-layerwise†	0.849	0.953	0.979	0.893	0.896
all	baseline	0.803	0.952	0.974	0.864	0.867
	MMKRF	**0.853**	0.965	**0.981**	**0.898**	**0.901**

Fusion. The fused retrieval results demonstrate superior performance compared to any single retrieval method, as shown in the "fusion" row of Table 1. Optimizing both sparse and dense retrieval is mutually beneficial, effectively improving recall performance in the fusion stage and generating higher-quality candidate sets. This approach even outperforms general-purpose re-ranking models with stronger semantic understanding across all metrics.

Re-ranking. As shown in the "reranker" row of Table 1, the re-ranking model exhibits strong semantic understanding capabilities, using it alone can yield decent retrieval results. Comparative experiments show that LLM-based re-ranking models outperform BERT-based ones in domain-specific scenarios, likely due to the LLM's richer pre-trained knowledge. After domain-adapted fine-tuning, the re-ranking model improves top-ranking performance but shows limited gains in recall, performing lower than fusion retrieval results and even the fine-tuned dense model on Recall@5. This underscores the distinct roles of retrieval stages: initial stages focus on efficient recall, while re-ranking emphasizes precise ordering. MMKRF uses the fine-tuned re-ranking model to sort the fusion stage's candidate set without filtering, enhancing relevant passages' rankings without sacrificing recall.

All. MMKRF optimizes each module effectively, achieving top results in every stage, as shown in the "all" row of Table 1. Compared to a general baseline, MMKRF boosts Accuracy by 5.0%, Recall@5 and MRR@5 by 1.3% and 3.4%, and Recall@10 and MRR@10 by 0.7% and 3.4%, respectively, showcasing its advanced performance in mechanics of materials knowledge retrieval.

6 Analysis

6.1 Domain Adaptation Optimization for Sparse Retrieval

Domain-specific vocabulary expansion and explicit knowledge enhancement both boost BM25's performance by strengthening term features. Ablation experiments confirm the effectiveness of each strategy, shown in Table 2. Both strategies improve BM25, and their effects are additive, with optimal performance when used together. However, as k increases, the gain from domain dictionary expansion on Recall@k diminishes, while explicit knowledge enhancement remains robust.

Table 2. Ablation study results of two optimization strategies for sparse retrieval on the MMCKR dataset.

Model	Acc	Recall@k				MRR@k	
		k = 3	k = 5	k = 7	k = 10	k = 5	k = 10
BM25_atire	0.705	0.855	0.912	0.937	0.953	0.785	0.791
with vocabulary	0.740	0.872	0.914	0.933	0.953	0.809	0.814
with knowledge	0.718	0.873	0.924	0.952	0.967	0.798	0.805
with both	**0.747**	**0.888**	**0.935**	**0.957**	**0.968**	**0.822**	**0.827**

6.2 Domain-Adaptive Fine-Tuning for Dense Retrieval Model

Data sampling, including method and quantity, is crucial for model training. Research shows hard negative sampling effectively learns discriminative features[26]. We use this method to generate negative samples by retrieving the top m knowledge passages with a re-ranking model, excluding ground truths, and using the rest as negatives. This increases the learning challenge during fine-tuning. First, we explored how sample quantity affects fine-tuning. As shown in Table 3, model performance improves with increasing m (4, 8, 16) but with diminishing returns, especially when m increases from 8 to 16. Larger sample quantities require the model to distinguish more texts simultaneously, increasing GPU memory usage, particularly with long texts.

To balance memory usage and model performance, we propose a **grouped sampling Strategy**: increasing the number of groups while keeping the in-group sample size small expands the total contrastive learning samples per query. Specifically, for each query, we sample two groups of hard negative samples, each containing 8 samples. We also test a **hybrid approach** (hardneg + random), combining one group of hard negatives with one group of random negatives to increase diversity. Results show that this multi-group strategy, particularly the hybrid approach, enhances model performance, as seen in Table 3. Mixed sampling reduces bias from single-strategy sampling and improves overall performance.

Table 3. Impact of sampling quantity and strategy on domain-adaptive fine-tuning for the dense retrieval model BGE-M3-Embedding. The evaluated sampling quantities are 4, 8, and 16. The symbol ' + ' represents grouped hybrid sampling strategies.

Model	m	*group*	Acc	Recall@k			MRR@k	
				$k = 3$	$k = 5$	$k = 10$	$k = 5$	$k = 10$
hardneg	4	1	0.801	0.912	0.941	0.965	0.859	0.862
hardneg	8	1	0.812	0.926	0.953	0.975	0.870	0.873
hardneg	16	1	0.811	0.924	0.954	0.974	0.870	0.872
hardneg	8	2	0.817	0.924	0.951	0.975	0.874	0.877
hardneg + random	8	2	**0.819**	**0.928**	**0.957**	**0.976**	**0.876**	**0.878**

6.3 Feasibility of Multi-Path Fusion Retrieval

We analyze retrieval results from BM25 and embedding models to quantify the consistency within and differences between these methods, and to assess the impact of domain adaptation optimization. For each query in the MMKRF test set, we gather the top 10 knowledge passages retrieved by each method and use the Jaccard similarity coefficient to measure differences between the sets.

A higher Jaccard similarity indicates a greater overlap between the two retrieval sets, which can be considered as consistency in the retrieval dimension. As shown in Fig. 2, BM25 variants show high consistency, with an average Jaccard similarity of 0.863 and 9 out of 10 identical passages, indicating robustness to parameter changes. Dense retrieval models have lower consistency, with an average similarity of 0.474 and about 6 overlapping passages, reflecting differences in semantic space modeling. After domain adaptation, BM25's consistency drops by 43.7% to a similarity of 0.563, with 7 overlapping passages. BGE-M3-Embedding's consistency drops by 62.9% to 0.371, with only half of the passages overlapping. This shows that domain adaptation significantly alters feature representations to better reflect domain-specific knowledge. The Jaccard similarity between sparse and dense retrieval is 0.318, highlighting their significant differences and strong complementarity, supporting multi-path fusion retrieval.

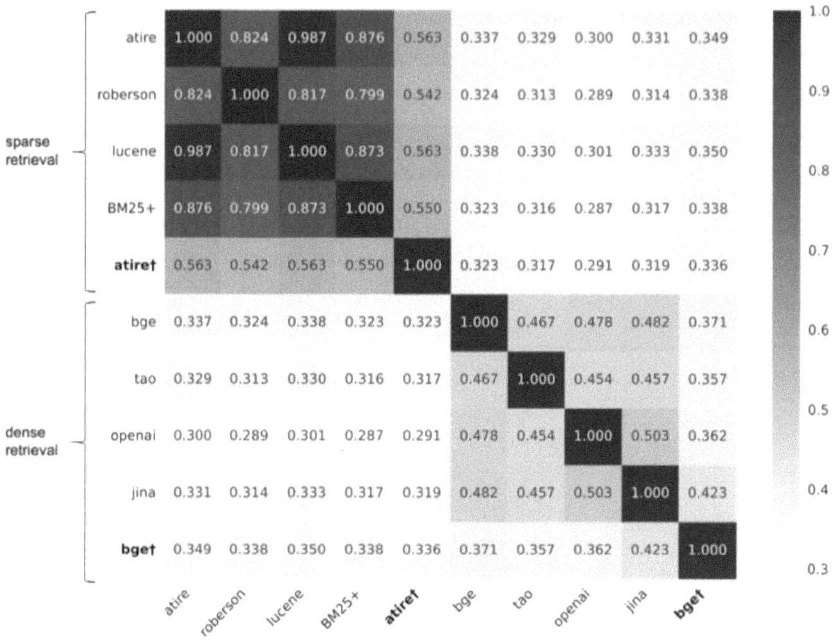

Fig. 2. Quantitative evaluation of the consistency of retrieval results among different retrieval algorithms and models, with bold indicating domain-adapted ones.

6.4 Selection of Optimal Fusion Algorithms

Common fusion methods include reciprocal rank fusion (RRF)[27] and linear weighted fusion (LWF). RRF combines results based on ranking positions, while LWF uses linear weighted fusion of relevance scores. Due to score scale differences, normalization (e.g., min-max, sigmoid) is often needed.

The fusion weight α is a key hyperparameter. Better-performing retrieval methods are typically assigned higher α values. Determining the optimal α is challenging. As shown in Table 4, compared to the other two fusion algorithms, LWF(sigmoid) achieves the best results across all metrics when $\alpha = 0.4$. Improper selection of α can degrade performance, especially for RRF and LWF (min-max), both of which underperform dense vector retrieval at $\alpha = 0.5$ in terms of Acc, shown in Fig. 3. Min-max normalization is highly sensitive to α and often yields worse results than pre-fusion due to its dispersed score distribution. Sigmoid normalization leads to more concentrated score distributions, resulting in more stable fusion outcomes.

Table 4. Performance comparison of three fusion algorithms on the MMCKR dataset, with optimal results achieved at $\alpha = 0.2$ for RRF, $\alpha = 0.1$ for LWF (min-max), and $\alpha = 0.4$ for LWF (sigmoid).

Model	Acc	Recall@k			MRR@k	
		$k = 3$	$k = 5$	$k = 10$	$k = 5$	$k = 10$
RRF_0.2	0.833	0.940	0.967	0.980	0.888	0.890
LWF(min-max)_0.1	0.844	0.948	0.966	0.981	0.895	0.898
LWF(sigmoid)_0.4	**0.845**	**0.950**	**0.968**	**0.981**	**0.897**	**0.899**

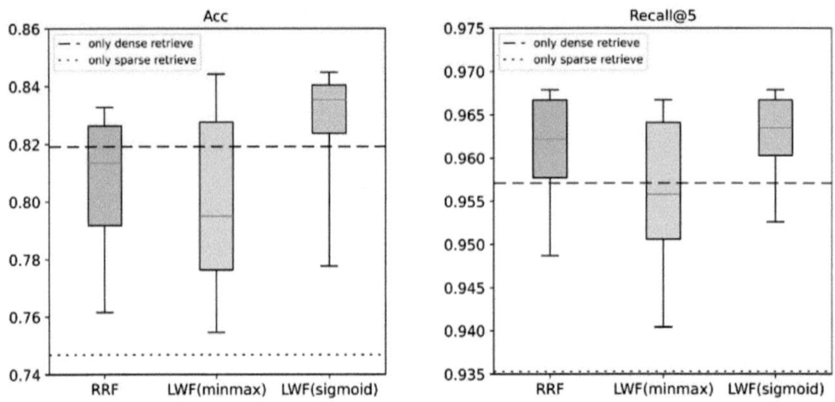

Fig. 3. Robustness comparison of three fusion algorithms as α varies between 0 and 1. The orange line denotes fusion results at $\alpha = 0.5$. For Acc, RRF outperforms pre-fusion only when $\alpha \in [0,0.4]$, LWF(min-max) when $\alpha \in [0,0.3]$, while LWF(sigmoid) consistently surpasses pre-fusion across $\alpha \in [0,0.7]$. For Recall@5, RRF performs better when $\alpha \in [0,0.7]$, LWF(min-max) when $\alpha \in [0,0.4]$, and LWF(sigmoid) remains superior for $\alpha \in [0,0.8]$, demonstrating its greater robustness to α variations.

6.5 Domain-Adaptive Fine-Tuning for Re-Ranking Model

Different model layers learn distinct features. Fine-tuning layers 8–40 of the re-ranking model shows that the middle layer (layer 24) performs best in MRR@5, as illustrated in Fig. 4.

We examine how sampling size and grouped sampling affect re-ranking. Using multi-path fusion, we retrieve the top 5 knowledge passages and re-rank them with the model. The best layer's results after training are compared, as shown in Table 5. Combining different sampling strategies in grouped sampling yields the best performance, confirming its effectiveness in domain-adapted fine-tuning, consistent with dense retrieval model findings (Sect. 6.2).

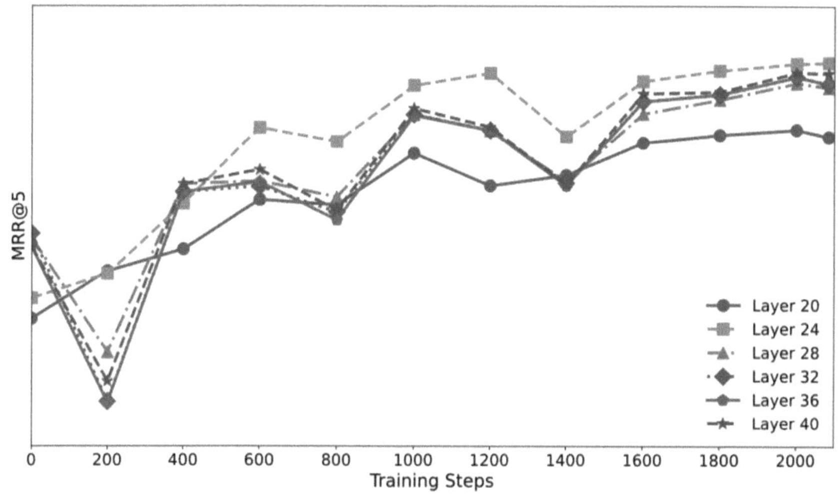

Fig. 4. Evolution of MRR@5 scores across layers in the MMKRF re-ranking model throughout training. Performance peaks at Layer 24.

Table 5. Impact of sampling quantity m and strategy on domain-adaptive fine-tuning for the re-ranking model. The evaluated sampling quantities are 4, 8, and 16. The symbol ' + ' represents grouped hybrid sampling strategies. The hybrid sampling selects the results from the 28th layer of the model, while all other sampling methods reach their best results at the 24th layer.

Model	*m*	*group*	Acc	Recall@2	Recall@3	MRR@5
hardneg	4	1	0.829	0.891	0.931	0.880
hardneg	8	1	0.831	0.894	0.932	0.882
hardneg	16	1	0.831	0.894	0.933	0.882
hardneg	8	2	0.831	0.899	0.933	0.883
hardneg + random	**8**	**2**	**0.838**	**0.899**	**0.935**	**0.887**

Prompts can enhance model performance by activating specific task and domain knowledge. We investigated the impact of prompts on a decoder-only model for text relevance scoring. The control group used a general prompt, experiment group 1 (specific) added domain-specific descriptions, and experiment group 2 (rewrite) completely restructured the prompt with detailed task instructions and domain context, more details in Table 6. All other training settings were kept consistent. Results in Table 7 show both experimental groups outperformed the control, with group 1 achieving the best results, proving the effectiveness of adding domain descriptions. Group 2's rewritten prompts differed too much from the pre-training prompts, causing a gap that limited improvement.

Table 6. The three types of prompts used for fine-tuning of the re-ranking model.

group	prompt
origin	Given a query A and a passage B, determine whether the passage contains an answer to the query by providing a prediction of either 'Yes' or 'No'
specific	You are responsible for determining the relationship between the query and the passage in the field of materials mechanics. Given a query A and a passage B, determine whether the passage contains an answer to the query by providing a prediction of either 'Yes' or 'No'
rewrite	Given a query A, which is a question or knowledge point in the field of materials mechanics, and a knowledge passage B in the field of materials mechanics, you need to determine whether the passage B contains an answer to the query A by providing a prediction of either 'Yes' or 'No'

Table 7. Impact of prompt design on domain-adaptive fine-tuning for the re-ranking model.

Model	Acc	Recall@2	Recall@3	MRR@5
origin	0.831	0.894	0.932	0.882
specific	**0.834**	**0.897**	0.931	**0.884**
rewrite	0.831	0.897	**0.934**	0.883

6.6 Application of Re-Ranking Models

Some post-retrieval methods merge and deduplicate candidate sets from different retrievals, then re-rank and filter them. MMKRF refines the ranking of weighted fusion-generated candidates while retaining all passages. As shown in Table 8, both merger and fusion improve retrieval performance compared to using only the re-ranker for retrieval, with fusion achieving better results. This shows that multi-path fusion provides higher-quality initial candidates, easing the re-ranker's burden and highlighting the fusion stage's importance. Further experiment shows that when the candidate set size in the fusion stage is reduced from Top 10 to Top 5, the top-ranking metrics improve further.

Table 8. Experimental results comparing two candidate set construction methods on the MMCKR dataset. The baseline uses only the fine-tuned re-ranking model.

Model	Acc	Recall@k			MRR@k	
		$k = 3$	$k = 5$	$k = 10$	$k = 5$	$k = 10$
reranker	0.849	0.935	0.953	0.979	0.893	0.896

(*continued*)

Table 8. (*continued*)

Model	Acc	Recall@k			MRR@k	
		$k = 3$	$k = 5$	$k = 10$	$k = 5$	$k = 10$
after merger (10)	0.851	0.940	0.955	**0.984**	0.893	0.896
after fusion (10)	0.853	0.944	0.965	0.981	0.898	**0.901**
after fusion (5)	**0.856**	**0.950**	**0.968**	-	**0.902**	-

7 Conclusion

In this paper, we propose MMKRF, a multi-stage knowledge retrieval framework for the field of mechanics of materials. We adapt and optimize the core algorithms and models within the framework to collaboratively enhance overall retrieval performance. Extensive ablation experiments demonstrate the effectiveness of all proposed optimization strategies. The superiority of MMKRF is validated through empirical experiments on the MMCKR dataset. Our work provides a reference for the design of retrieval frameworks and domain adaptation research in specialized fields.

Acknowledgments. This work was supported by the Beijing Forestry University Artificial Intelligence Demonstration Course Pilot Construction Project (BJFU2024RGZN25).

References

1. Huang, L., et al.: A survey on hallucination in large language models: principles, taxonomy, challenges, and open questions. arXiv preprint arXiv:2311.05232 (2023)
2. Peng, B., et al.: Check your facts and try again: improving large language models with external knowledge and automated feedback. arXiv preprint arXiv:2302.12813 (2023)
3. Lewis, P., et al.: Retrieval-augmented generation for knowledge-intensive NLP tasks. In: Proceedings of the 34th International Conference on Neural Information Processing Systems, pp. Article 793. Curran Associates Inc., Vancouver, BC, Canada (2020)
4. Izacard, G., Grave, E.: Leveraging passage retrieval with generative models for open domain question answering. arXiv preprint arXiv:2007.01282 (2020)
5. Ram, O., et al.: In-context retrieval-augmented language models. Trans. Assoc. Comput. Ling. **11**, 1316–1331 (2023)
6. Wu, J., et al.: CoRAL: collaborative retrieval-augmented large language models improve long-tail recommendation. In: Proceedings of the 30th ACM SIGKDD Conference on Knowledge Discovery and Data Mining, pp. 3391–3401. Association for Computing Machinery, Barcelona, Spain (2024)
7. Chen, J., Lin, H., Han, X., Sun, L.: Benchmarking large language models in retrieval-augmented generation. In: Proceedings of the AAAI Conference on Artificial Intelligence, pp. 17754–17762. (2024)
8. Yoran, O., Wolfson, T., Ram, O., Berant, J.: Making retrieval-augmented language models robust to irrelevant context. arXiv preprint arXiv:2310.01558 (2023)

9. Maekawa, S., Iso, H., Gurajada, S., Bhutani, N.: Retrieval helps or hurts? A deeper dive into the efficacy of retrieval augmentation to language models. arXiv preprint arXiv:2402.13492 (2024)
10. Liu, N.F., et al.: Lost in the middle: how language models use long contexts. arXiv preprint arXiv:2307.03172 (2023)
11. Feng, Z., Kuang, D., Wang, Z., Nie, Z., Zheng, Y., Zhang, R.: EasyRAG: efficient retrieval-augmented generation framework for automated network operations. arXiv preprint arXiv: 2410.10315 (2024)
12. Lozano, A., Fleming, S.L., Chiang, C.-C., Shah, N.: Clinfo. AI: An open-source retrieval-augmented large language model system for answering medical questions using scientific literature. In: PACIFIC SYMPOSIUM ON BIOCOMPUTING 2024, pp. 8–23. World Scientific, (2023)
13. Ramos, J.: Using TF-IDF to determine word relevance in document queries. In: Proceedings of the First Instructional Conference on Machine Learning, pp. 29–48. Citeseer, (2003)
14. Robertson, S., Zaragoza, H.: The probabilistic relevance framework: BM25 and beyond. Found. Trends® Info. Retr. **3**, 333–389 (2009)
15. Reimers, N., Gurevych, I.: Sentence-BERT: sentence embeddings using siamese bert-networks. arXiv preprint arXiv:1908.10084 (2019)
16. Gao, T., Yao, X., Chen, D.: SimCSE: simple contrastive learning of sentence embeddings. arXiv preprint arXiv:2104.08821 (2021)
17. Chen, J., Xiao, S., Zhang, P., Luo, K., Lian, D., Liu, Z.: BGE M3-Embedding: Multi-lingual, multi-functionality, multi-granularity text embeddings through self-knowledge distillation. arXiv preprint arXiv:2402.03216 (2024)
18. Reichman, B., Heck, L.: Dense passage retrieval: is it retrieving? arXiv preprint arXiv:2402.11035 (2024)
19. Karpukhin, V., et al.: Dense passage retrieval for open-domain question answering. In: Association for Computational Linguistics, pp. 6769–6781 (2020)
20. Gao, L., Ma, X., Lin, J., Callan, J.: Precise zero-shot dense retrieval without relevance labels. In: Association for Computational Linguistics, pp. 1762–1777 (2023)
21. Ma, X., Gong, Y., He, P., Zhao, H., Duan, N.: Query rewriting in retrieval-augmented large language models. In: Proceedings of the 2023 Conference on Empirical Methods in Natural Language Processing, pp. 5303–5315. (2023)
22. Borgeaud, S., et al.: Improving language models by retrieving from trillions of tokens. In: International Conference on Machine Learning, pp. 2206–2240. PMLR, (2022)
23. Wang, Y., Li, P., Sun, M., Liu, Y.: Self-knowledge guided retrieval augmentation for large language models. In: Association for Computational Linguistics, pp. 10303–10315 (2023)
24. Kamphuis, C., De Vries, A.P., Boytsov, L., Lin, J.: Which BM25 do you mean? A large-scale reproducibility study of scoring variants. In: Advances in Information Retrieval: 42nd European Conference on IR Research, ECIR 2020, Lisbon, Portugal, April 14–17, 2020, Proceedings, Part II 42, pp. 28–34. Springer, (2020)
25. Hu, E.J., et al.: Lora: low-rank adaptation of large language models. ICLR **1**, 3 (2022)
26. Zhou, K., et al.: SimANS: simple ambiguous negatives sampling for dense text retrieval. In: Association for Computational Linguistics, pp. 548–559 (2022)
27. Cormack, G.V., Clarke, C.L.A., Buettcher, S.: Reciprocal rank fusion outperforms Condorcet and individual rank learning methods. In: Proceedings of the 32nd international ACM SIGIR Conference on Research and Development in Information Retrieval, pp. 758–759. Association for Computing Machinery, Boston, MA, USA (2009)

Multi-round Dialogue Embedding Based on Dynamic Context Awareness

Jian Ni[1], Zhiyu Zheng[1], and Zhao Cao[2(✉)]

[1] School of Smart Governance, Renmin University of China, Suzhou, China
{nijian191,zhiyu}@ruc.edu.cn

[2] Gaoling School of Artificial Intelligence, Renmin University of China, Beijing, China
caozhao@ruc.edu.cn

Abstract. In recent years, with the rapid development of LLMs, agent and RAG technologies, multi-round human-computer interaction applications increasingly require efficient retrieval of dialogue content to understand user intent and generate coherent responses. However, existing methods mostly rely on fixed windows or single-round dialogue embeddings, which struggle to dynamically adapt to context changes, suffering from issues such as information truncation, information noise, and no-explicit semantic associations. To address these challenges, this paper proposes a dynamic context-aware embedding method, which leverages LLMs to infer the relevant historical range associated with the current utterance, filters highly related dialogue content through semantic matching, and generates natural language instructions to explicitly model cross-round semantic chains. Experiments demonstrate that this method significantly outperforms traditional embedding approaches on the LoCoMo dataset and exhibits strong robustness across various dialogue scenarios. This work provides new ideas and practical approaches for building intelligent agent systems with semantic understanding and dynamic memory capabilities.

Keywords: Dynamic Context Awareness · Dialogue Retrieval · LLM-based Semantic Modeling

1 Introduction

In recent years, applications powered by large language models (LLMs), autonomous agents and RAG [8,9] have witnessed rapid development. These technologies are being widely deployed across various domains, including question answering systems, intelligent customer service, educational tutoring, and e-commerce platforms. A common feature of such systems is their engagement in multi-round interactions between human users and AI models [16], where the interaction patterns exhibit strong contextual dependencies and semantic continuity.

Z. Li et al. (Eds.): CCIR 2025, LNCS 16369, pp. 119–132, 2026.
https://doi.org/10.1007/978-981-95-5637-3_9

In the context of multi-round dialogues, accurately understanding user intent and effectively completing tasks requires the system to rely on a memory mechanism [17] to dynamically store and manage historical conversational content. An effective memory mechanism must not only retain the information exchanged in each turn but also support precise retrieval of relevant historical content in response to new user queries. This capability is critical for several key functions, including user intent modeling, personalized response generation, task trajectory tracking, and information completion.

Notably, in multi-round dialogue retrieval scenarios, the modeling of cross-round semantic associations emerges as a central challenge [10]. For instance, in an e-commerce customer service setting, a user may inquire about the technical specifications of a product in earlier turns and later shift the topic to after-sales policies. In such cases, the system must be capable of maintaining accurate linkage to the product discussed earlier, even during topic transitions, in order to ensure contextual coherence and content relevance in its responses.

In the field of information retrieval, a common approach is to segment the corpus into fixed-size chunks and then compute embeddings [6,18]. We call it here the fixed-window embedding method. However, such chunk-based methods face significant limitations when applied to multi-round dialogues. It often struggle to balance information completeness and noise suppression, as fixed-window sizes cannot dynamically adapt to the complexity of dialogue structures. This may lead to either the loss of critical information or the inclusion of irrelevant content that degrades retrieval performance. We summarizes the issues of this method as follows: **Information Truncation**, **Information Noise**, **Non-explicit Semantic Associations**. Multi-round dialogue retrieval is a domain-specific retrieval task, yet existing studies have rarely focused on learning contextualized embeddings that dynamically incorporate relevant dialogue history. In many LLM and agent-based memory systems—such as MemoryBank [19], MemGPT [12] and Mem0 [3]—dialogue turns are embedded individually and stored as long-term memory entries for later retrieval. Despite these advances, such approaches remain limited by their static treatment of context and their shallow semantic representation capabilities.

To overcome the limitations of existing methods, we propose an embedding approach based on dynamic context awareness. The proposed framework consists of three key components: **Dynamic Window Selector**, **Window Refiner**, and **Context Generator**. Dynamic Window Selector leverages a LLM to infer the relevant historical context for the current utterance, replacing the traditional fixed-window strategy. This allows the system to dynamically adapt to varying contextual dependencies and avoid the limitations of static context configurations. Window Refiner employs a semantic matching model to further filter the retrieved dialogue history, retaining only highly relevant utterances. This step suppresses noise introduced by irrelevant content and enhances the semantic purity of the final embedding. Context Generator uses the LLM to produce natural language instructions that explicitly activate logical chains across dialogue turns. This promotes deeper semantic association and improves representation learning for complex multi-round scenarios. Compared to traditional embedding approaches, our method demonstrates superior retrieval performance in multi-round dialogue settings and exhibits enhanced robustness across diverse conversational contexts.

The main contributions of this paper are as follows:

- We identify and formalize three key challenges in multi-round dialogue retrieval: *Information Truncation*, *Information Noise*, and *Non-explicit Semantic Associations*.
- We propose a novel embedding framework based on dynamic context awareness, comprising three core components—*Dynamic Window Selector*, *Window Refiner*, and *Context Generator*—each targeting one of the aforementioned challenges to enhance context-aware semantic representations.
- Extensive experiments on the LoCoMo [11] dataset demonstrate that our method outperforms traditional static embedding approaches and exhibits strong robustness across various dialogue scenarios.

The rest of this paper is organized as follows: Sect. 2 reviews related work from the perspectives of retrieval methods and multi-round dialogue retrieval. Section 3 defines the key challenges in multi-round dialogue scenarios. Section 4 presents our proposed method in detail, including its overall design and core components. Section 5 reports and analyzes the experimental results. Finally, Sect. 6 concludes the paper and outlines directions for future work.

2 Related Work

Retrieval Methods can be categorized into two types according to the retrieval representation: sparse retrieval and dense retrieval [6]. Existing retrieval methods mainly comprise the following phases: a first phase generates a retrieval representation by a retriever, a second phase generates an index of the retrieval representation for efficient retrieval, and a third phase searches the slowed down representation according to the retrieval target and returns TopK retrieved content. Sparse retrieval methods leverage term matching metrics such as TF-IDF [1] and BM25 [14], which analyze word statistics from texts and construct inverted indices for efficient searching. Unlike sparse retrieval, dense retrieval methods represent queries and keys using dense embedding vectors. For text data, recent advances in pre-trained models (such as BERT [4]) have been employed to encode queries and keys individually. This approach is often referred to as **Dense Passage Retrieval** (DPR [7]). Similarly to text, models have been proposed to encode code data, audio data, image data, video data, etc. [18]

Multi-round Dialogue Retrieval. refers to the process of retrieving content from historical dialogues related to the query. With the rapid development of Agent applications, there is an urgent need for the development of memory mechanisms to work with them. In multi-round dialogue domain, dialogue memories are usually retrieved in the form of RAG, which are used to enhance the LLM's knowledge of the user to accomplish tasks that are more relevant to the user's role. Existing dialogue memories contain, on the one hand, rule-based Persona knowledge, which is a synopsis of the dialogue content according to a certain rule framework during multiple rounds of Dialogues, e.g., MemGPT [12], MemoryBank [19]. And on the other hand, dialogue memories contain the original dialogue content, e.g., Generative Agents [13], Mem0 [3], which embeddings dialogues and let LLM decides whether to retrieve the dialogues content in current context. In terms of original dialogue content retrieval, existing methods still adopt the paradigm of dense retrieval to embedding the content of Role monologue dialog without considering the contextual support provided by the context for the current content under multi-round dialogue. This approach is flawed in scenarios like multi-round dialogues where the context is continuous and relevant.

3 Probelm Statement

This section first analyzes the issues of multi-round dialogue retrieval and then presents the problems to be solved in this paper based on the results of the analysis.

3.1 Issues in Multi-round Dialogue Retrieval

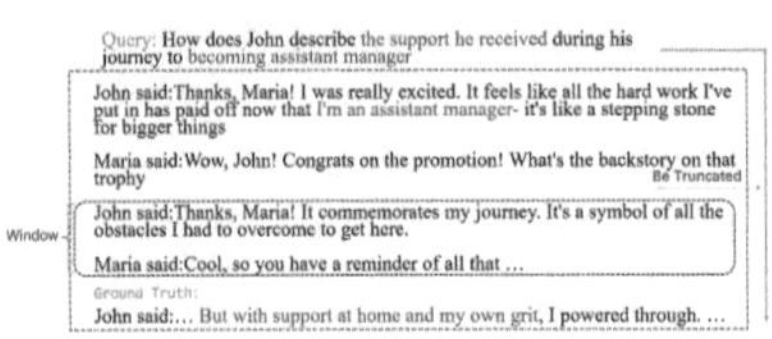

(a) Information Truncation Example

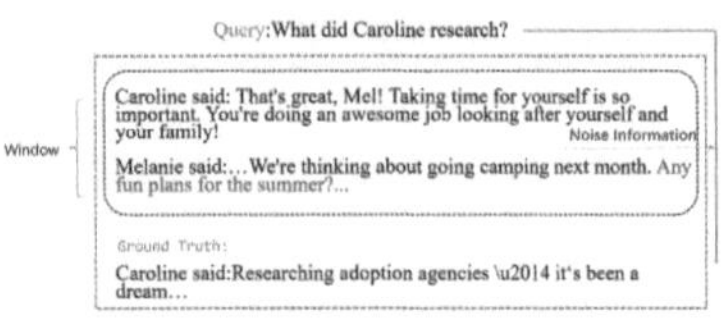

(b) Information Noise Example

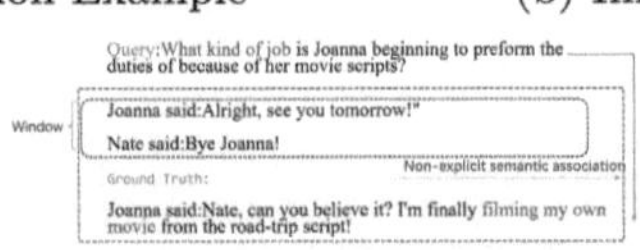

(c) Non-explicit Semantic Associations Example

Fig. 1. Three types of issue examples from the retrieval output

Taking the LoCoMo [11] dataset as an example, we analyzes in depth and proposes three types of issues of traditional methods in multi-round dialogues retrieval as follows:

Information Truncation. Figure 1 a reveals fixed window truncates the continuity of the conversation, resulting in an incomplete conversation. Also, some of the references in the current dialogue come from outside the window, and the references of some entities are not clear.

Information Noise. Illustrated in Fig. 1 b Multiple topics in the window content, interference between topics, and topic shifting in the current dialog content.

Non-explicit Semantic Associations. Figure 1 c shows that there are non-explicit semantic associations between the window content and the utterance, e.g., there is no clear entity designation; or the current dialogue content is logically related to the query, and it is difficult to express such semantic associations in an explicit method.

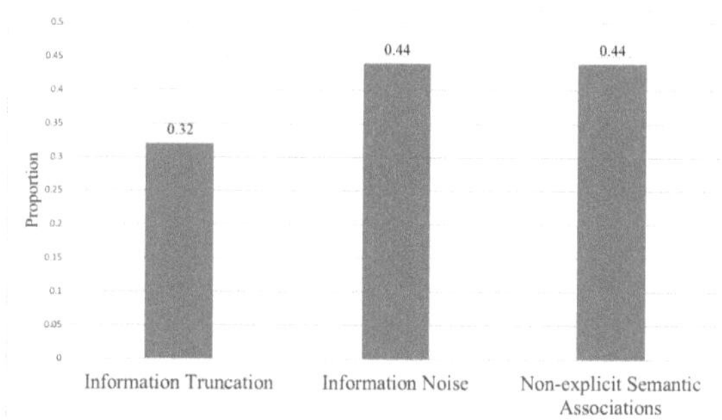

Fig. 2. Proportion of Different Issues

We sampled from LoCoMo and made statistics on the three types of issues in Fig. 2. The issues of *Information Noise* and *Non-explicit Semantic Associations* are more significant, with a proportion of 44% and 46% respectively, and the *Information Truncation* has a relatively small proportion of 32%.

3.2 Problem Formulation and Key Definitions

Notations

We consider a multi-round dialogue process between two parties, represented as a sequence:

$$[U_1, S_1, U_2, S_2, \ldots, U_n, S_n] \tag{1}$$

where U_i and S_i denote the utterances from the two participants (e.g., User and System) in the i-th turn, and n is the total number of dialogue turns.

Each user utterance U_i is composed of a sequence of sentences:

$$U_i = [t_1^{U_i}, t_2^{U_i}, \ldots, t_k^{U_i}] \tag{2}$$

where $t_j^{U_i}$ denotes the j-th sentence in U_i, and $1 \leq j \leq k$.

Similarly, the system utterance S_i is defined as:

$$S_i = [t_1^{S_i}, t_2^{S_i}, \dots, t_l^{S_i}], \tag{3}$$

where $t_j^{S_i}$ denotes the j-th sentence in S_i, and $1 \leq j \leq l$.

Each $t_j^{U_i}$ and $t_j^{S_i}$ represents a single sentence, which serves as the atomic unit of the dialogue content.

Dynamic Context-aware Embedding. For a given utterance U_i (or S_i), we consider a fixed-size dialogue context window of length MAX_WINDOW, which includes the preceding turns:

$$[U_{i-\text{MAX\_WINDOW}}, S_{i-\text{MAX\_WINDOW}}, \dots, U_{i-1}, S_{i-1}]. \tag{4}$$

Within this window, we search for the earliest turn index m such that the subsequence

$$[U_m, S_m, U_{m+1}, S_{m+1}, \dots, U_{i-1}, S_{i-1}] \tag{5}$$

provides sufficient contextual support for understanding U_i.

From this selected window, we extract key information relevant to U_i, defined as:

$$\text{KeyInfo} = \{t \mid t \in U_p \,\text{or}\, t \in S_q,\ m \leq p, q \leq i-1\}. \tag{6}$$

A context representation is then generated based on the extracted key information and the current utterance:

$$\text{Context} = \text{Gen}(\text{KeyInfo}, U_i). \tag{7}$$

We concatenate the context with the current utterance to obtain:

$$[\text{Context}, U_i]. \tag{8}$$

Specifically, given a query embedding Q and its target utterance U_i, we aim to ensure:

$$\text{Sim}\left(Q,\ \text{Embedding}([\text{Context}, U_i])\right) \geq \text{Sim}\left(Q,\ \text{Embedding}([U_i])\right), \tag{9}$$

here $\text{Sim}(\cdot, \cdot)$ denotes a similarity function (e.g., cosine similarity), and $\text{Embedding}(\cdot)$ denotes the embedding function applied to the input sequence.

4 Methodology

In this section we present our dynamic context-aware embedding approach. As shown in Fig. 3, our method contains three main parts:

Dynamic Window Selector: Based on the current utterance, we use LLM to infer about the appropriate context window. This part dynamically selects the

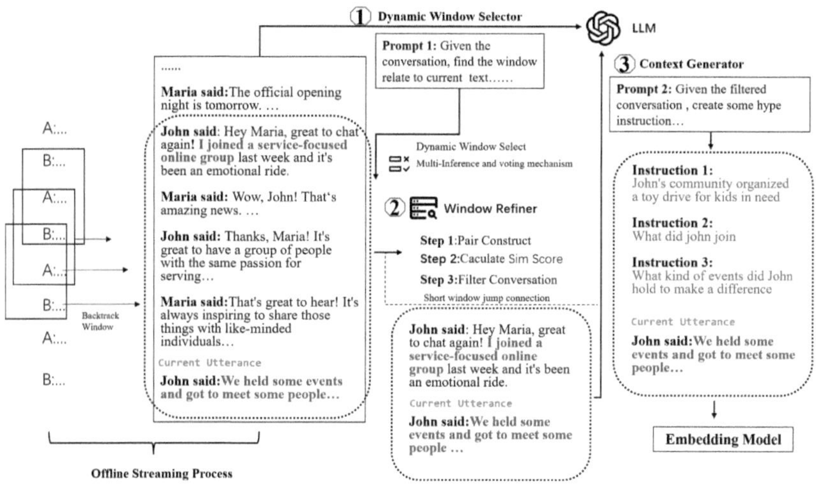

Fig. 3. Framework for Dynamic Context-Aware Embedding

window size by LLM. LLM performs context-aware dialogue content, efficiently reasoning and dynamically delimiting the most relevant historical dialogue window boundaries for the current utterance. The principle of window selection is as follows:

(1) **Semantic Continuity**: there is a clear semantic correlation between the content of the dialogue in the window and the current utterance, avoiding information truncation and noise amplification.
(2) **Theme Consistency**: the dialogue content in the window is centered around the topic of the current utterance, avoiding the interference of multi-topic mixing.
(3) **Referential Clarity**: clear referential relationships in the content of dialogue within the window, avoiding the ambiguity of long-dependent entity referentials.
(4) **Logical Relationships**: logical relationships exist between the content of the dialogues in the window and the current utterance, avoiding the omission of non-display semantic dependencies.

Furthermore, to mitigate the output uncertainty of Large Language Models (LLMs), a multi-inference, voting, and fallback mechanism is employed when leveraging LLMs for window inference. Specifically, for each dialogue data instance, multiple candidate windows are generated through multi-round inference, and the frequency of each window across these rounds is taken as its confidence score. A window is deemed valid if its confidence score exceeds a predefined threshold; otherwise, the process falls back to the fixed-window strategy.

Window Refiner: Based on the current utterance, we use the reranker model to filter the seleced window content for noise reduction purpose.To further refine the contextual window, we perform a semantic relevance evaluation between the current utterance U_i and each utterance within the selected window.

Specifically, for each j such that $i - m \leq j \leq i - 1$, m denotes the selected window index, we construct pairs (U_i, X_j), where $X_j \in \{U_j, S_j\}$, representing either participant's utterance at turn j.

For each pair, we compute the semantic similarity score:

$$\text{Sim}(U_i, X_j) \tag{10}$$

where $\text{Sim}(\cdot, \cdot)$ denotes a predefined similarity function (e.g., cosine similarity over embeddings).

We then compare each similarity score against a threshold τ. The utterance X_j is retained if:

$$\text{Sim}(U_i, X_j) \geq \tau \tag{11}$$

All utterances x_j satisfying the threshold condition constitute the refined context:

$$\text{Refined Context} = \{X_j \mid \text{Sim}(U_i, X_j) \geq \tau,\ i - m \leq j \leq i - 1\} \tag{12}$$

Context Generator: Based on the current utterance U_i and the refined window, we leverage a LLM to generate a set of *hypothetical instructions.*

Inspired by prior work HYDE [5] of generating hypothetical documents to improve retrieval, we propose generating hypothetical instructions tailored to multi-round dialogue settings.

In our setup, a hypothetical instruction is a natural-language query, explanation, or clue that is: (1) explicitly grounded in the current utterance U_i, (2) informed by the refined window, (3) or semantically aligned with the underlying intent or topic of utterance

These instructions aim to surface implicit semantic links between the current utterance and refined window, thereby making such relationships explicit at the representation level. The generated instructions serve to enrich the information content of U_i, and can be used to enhance downstream retrieval or reasoning tasks. Table 1 shows the three main types of hypothetical instructions to extract implicit semantic associations from the three dimensions of Coreference Resolution, Logical Inference, and Emotional Continuation.

5 Experiments

5.1 Experimental Setup

Datasets. We conduct experiments on the LoCoMo [11] dataset, which contains samples of multi-round dialogues across domains, with an average of 300

Table 1. Types of Semantic Bridging Templates and Examples

Template Type	Generation Pattern	Example
Coreference Resolution	Entity linking + pronoun disambiguation	What does "it" refer to in the current utterance?
Logical Inference	Causal chain construction + temporal ordering	Why does the protagonist go play football in the current utterance?
Emotional Continuation	Emotion transition + intent prediction	How does the protagonist feel after seeing the kitten?

interactions and 9000 tokens per multi-round conversation, covering e-commerce inquiries, daily chit-chat, and professional QA scenarios, with a total of 35 conversation sessions. We evaluate the retrieval effectiveness using the LoCoMo QA test set, which contains more than 1,200 multi-round dialogue query-response pairs, where each query is labeled with the dialog content associated with the query.

Comparison Methods. We compare two distinct utterance embedding strategies: the first is a static single-utterance embedding approach, in which each utterance is embedded independently without incorporating any prior context. The second approach enhances the current utterance representation by concatenating it with a fixed-size window of preceding dialogue turns, thereby incorporating contextual information from earlier interactions. We call this method as fixed-window embedding approach. In our proposed method, both the *Dynamic Window Selector* and the *Context Generator* components utilize the Llama-3.3-70B-Instruct [15], while the *Window Refiner* is implemented using the BGE-M3-Reranker [2]. All methods employ the same underlying embedding model, BGE-M3 [2], ensuring that any observed differences in performance are attributable solely to variations in contextual processing strategies.

Evaluation Settings. We use Recall@5 as the main evaluation metric, which measures the proportion of relevant samples retrieved among the top 5 results. It is defined as:

$$\text{Recall@5} = \frac{\text{Relevant Samples in Top 5}}{\text{Ground Truth samples}} \times 100\% \tag{13}$$

5.2 Experimental Results

5.2.1 Main Results

As shown in Fig. 4, the single-utterance embedding approach achieves a Recall@5 of 58%. The fixed-window embedding approach performs better with a window size of 1 or 2, reaching a Recall@5 of 61% at window size 1. However, as the window size increases further, performance declines. This indicates that short context windows provide useful semantic support for the current utterance, helping to mitigate the issue of semantic fragmentation in isolated embeddings and thereby improving retrieval effectiveness. In contrast, larger context windows

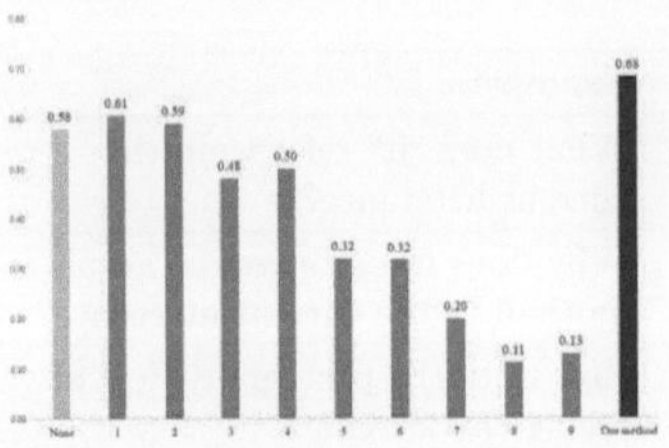

Fig. 4. Performance comparison of different methods

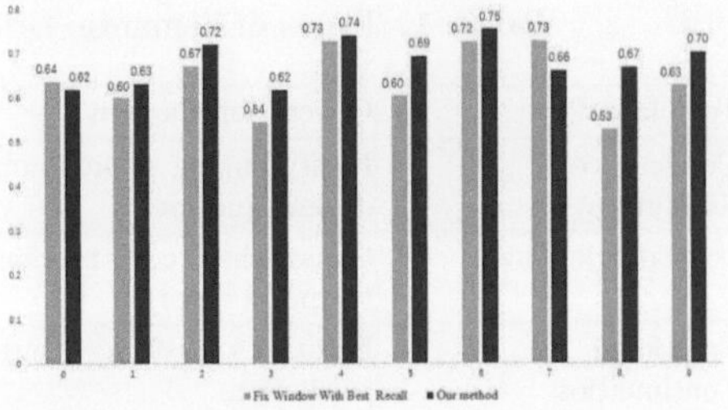

Fig. 5. Performance comparison of the fixed-window embedding approach (window size = 1) and our method

introduce excessive irrelevant information, leading to a noise amplification effect that ultimately harms retrieval performance. Our proposed method achieves a Recall@5 of 68%, outperforming the fixed-window embedding approach (61% at window size 2) by 7% points and the single-utterance approach (58%) by 10% points, demonstrating the effectiveness of our dynamic context-aware strategy.

Figure 5 compares the Recall@5 performance of the fixed-window embedding approach (window size = 1) and our proposed method across various multi-round dialogues in the test set. It is evident that our method outperforms the fixed-window approach in the majority of dialogue cases, with the maximum improvement reaching up to 12%. Moreover, the standard deviation of Recall@5 across different dialogues is 0.049 for our method, compared to 0.073 for the fixed-window embedding approach—representing a reduction of approximately 32%. This result demonstrates that our method exhibits greater robustness and stability across diverse dialogue scenarios.

Figure 6 presents the distribution of optimal fixed window sizes that yield the highest Recall@5 for each dialogue when using the fixed-window embedding approach. In contrast, Fig. 7 shows the predicted window sizes for each utterance generated by our proposed method. As revealed in Fig. 6, different dialogues achieve their best recall performance at different window sizes, indicating that a globally fixed window size fails to generalize across diverse dialogue types or domains. This highlights the limited adaptability of fixed-window strategies when applied to the evolving dialogues. In practice, the need for contextual information varies across dialogue content, making it necessary to adjust the window size dynamically based on the current utterance.Fig. 7 further demonstrates that our method selects a wide range of window sizes, which significantly diverges from the optimal distribution observed for the fixed-window approach. This result underscores the generalization ability of our model, as it can adaptively capture context across varying dialogue scenarios.

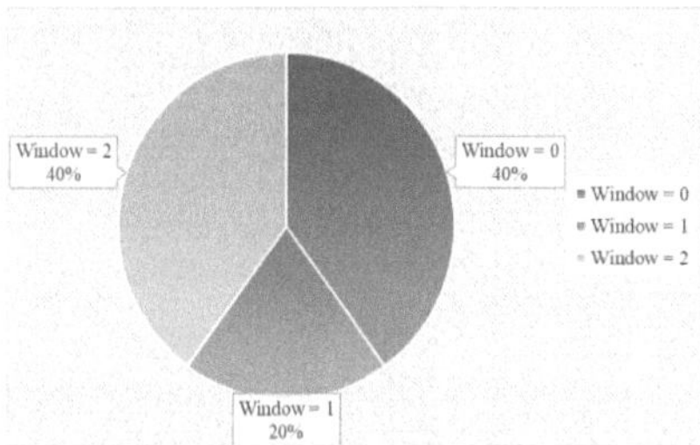

Fig. 6. Distribution of Window size of fixed-window approach

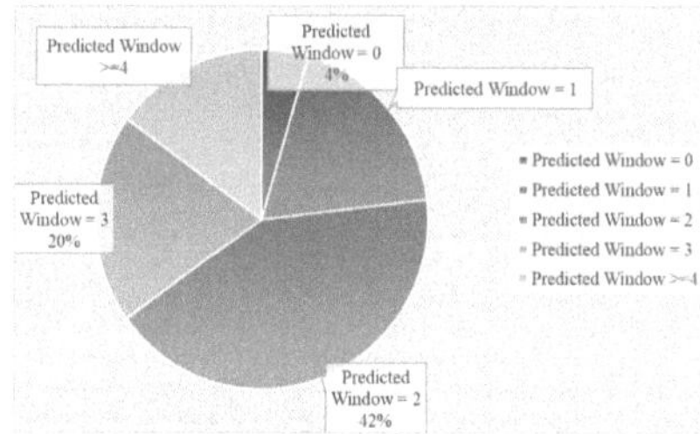

Fig. 7. Distribution of Predicted window size of our method

5.2.2 Case Study

For three key issues proposed in Sect. 3, our method successfully retrieves relevant utterances in all corresponding cases. The retrieval outcomes of the three representative examples are illustrated in Fig. 8. Specifically, Fig. 8 (a), (b), and (c) correspond to the examples discussed in Fig. 1 (a), (b), and (c), respectively.

For the *Information Truncation* issue, Fig. 8 (a) demonstrates that our method dynamically identifies a context window of size 4 for the target utterance, which successfully covers the critical information "assistant manager." This adaptive window selection effectively prevents semantic truncation.

In Fig. 8 (b), the predicted context window size is 0, indicating that no historical utterance is necessary for representing the target utterance. This setting avoids introducing irrelevant contextual noise, which might otherwise degrade semantic representation.

Figure 8 (c) shows that our method selects a context window size of 4, thus incorporating rich preceding dialogue information. Among the retrieved instructions, Instruction 1 and Instruction 2 contain key phrases such as "movie scripts" and "filming her own movie," which are semantically related to the query and help to establish a meaningful connection between the query and the target utterance.

5.2.3 Ablation Study

To validate the effectiveness of the three modules proposed in this paper, an ablation study was conducted in this section. As shown in 9, we progressively removed the *Window Refiner* and *Dynamic Window Selector* from the baseline configuration of our method. The results indicate that the performance degrades as modules are sequentially removed. Notably, the configuration with only the Context Generator module outperforms the fixed-window baseline significantly, suggesting that this module contributes the most to the overall improvement. The other two modules provide complementary enhancements to the Context Generator.

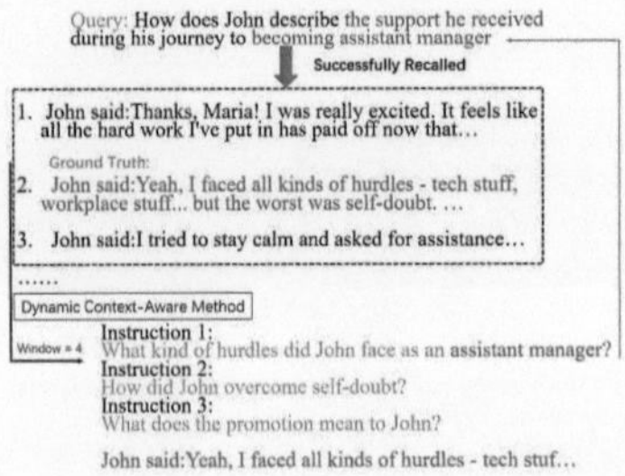

(a) Information Truncation Example

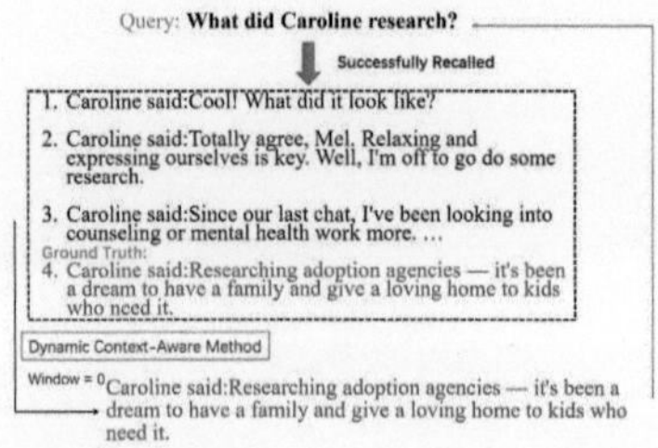

(b) Information Noise Example

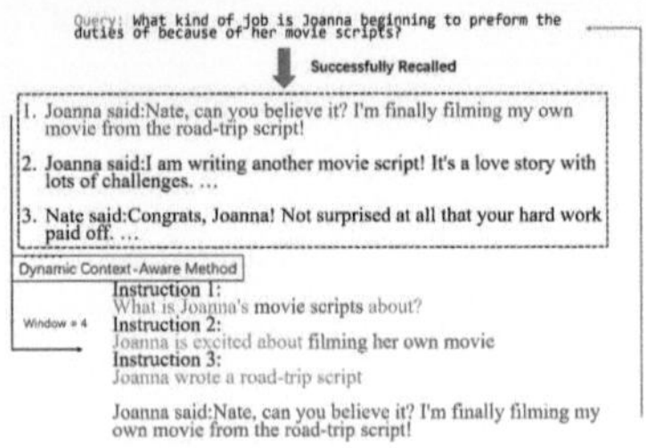

(c) Non-explicit Semantic Associations Example

Fig. 8. Three examples of mitigation issues

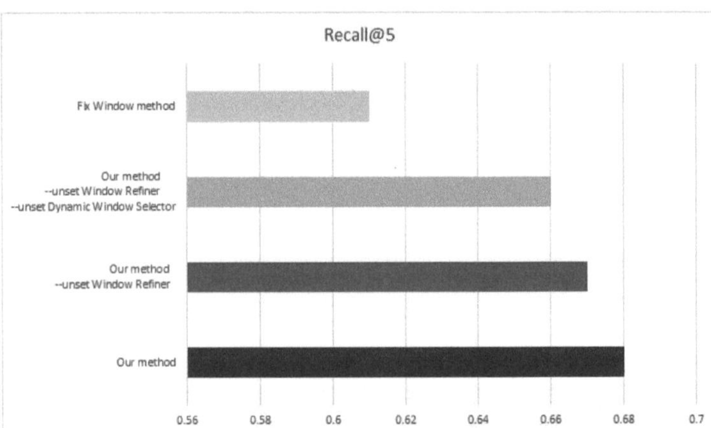

Fig. 9. Ablation Study

6 Conclusion and Future Work

In this article, we propose a dynamic context-aware embedding optimization framework for multi-round dialogue retrieval, addressing several critical challenges in existing methods, including *Information Truncation*, *Information Noise*, and *Non-explicit Semantic Associations*. Our approach integrates three key modules: *Dynamic Window Selector*, *Window Refiner*, and *Context Generator*. Through their joint operation, the framework achieves intelligent modeling and semantic enhancement of dialogue history.

Retrieval Performance. Experimental results on the LoCoMo dataset demonstrate that our method achieves a Recall@5 of 63%, outperforming the best-performing fixed-window embedding approach (61%) by 2%, and the static single-utterance baseline (58%) by 5%. Notably, in 50% of the test dialogues, our method yields over 5% improvement in recall compared to the fixed-window approach, with the maximum observed gain reaching 12%.

Robustness. The variance of Recall@5 across different dialogue scenarios is 0.0029, representing a 40% reduction compared to the fixed-window approach (0.0048). This indicates enhanced robustness and generalization capability across diverse conversation contexts. Moreover, the dynamically selected window sizes span a broad range, further supporting its adaptability.

While our method demonstrates promising advances in dynamic context modeling, several directions remain open for future exploration: (1)we aim to reduce computational overhead by incorporating lightweight architectures (e.g., retrieval-augmented small models or adapter-based modules) and dynamic inference techniques (e.g., conditional computation, attention pruning). (2)We plan to enhance real-time adaptability by integrating intent tracking mechanisms to capture evolving user intentions. (3) To improve interpretability, we will explore visualization tools and causal reasoning frameworks for explaining window selection and semantic alignment.

Acknowledgements. This work was supported by the Suzhou Key Laboratory of Artificial Intelligence and Social Governance Technologies under Grant No. SZS2023007, and the Smart Social Governance Technology and Innovative Application Platform of Suzhou Dushu Lake Science and Education Innovation Zone under Grant No. YZCXPT2023101. The authors would like to express their sincere gratitude for the financial support provided by these projects.

References

1. On relevance weights with little relevance information. ACM Sigir Forum (2007)
2. Chen, J., Xiao, S., Zhang, P., Luo, K., Lian, D., Liu, Z.: BGE M3-embedding: multi-lingual, multi-functionality, multi-granularity text embeddings through self-knowledge distillation (2024). https://arxiv.org/abs/2402.03216
3. Chhikara, P., Khant, D., Aryan, S., Singh, T., Yadav, D.: Mem0: building production-ready AI agents with scalable long-term memory (2025). https://arxiv.org/abs/2504.19413
4. Devlin, J., Chang, M.W., Lee, K., Toutanova, K.: Bert: pre-training of deep bidirectional transformers for language understanding (2019). https://arxiv.org/abs/1810.04805
5. Gao, L., Ma, X., Lin, J., Callan, J.: Precise zero-shot dense retrieval without relevance labels (2022). https://arxiv.org/abs/2212.10496

6. Gao, Y., et al.: Retrieval-augmented generation for large language models: a survey (2024). https://arxiv.org/abs/2312.10997
7. Karpukhin, V., et al.: Dense passage retrieval for open-domain question answering (2020). https://arxiv.org/abs/2004.04906
8. Lewis, P., et al.: Retrieval-augmented generation for knowledge-intensive NLP tasks (2021). https://arxiv.org/abs/2005.11401
9. Liu, B., et al.: Advances and challenges in foundation agents: from brain-inspired intelligence to evolutionary, collaborative, and safe systems (2025). https://arxiv.org/abs/2504.01990
10. Ma, X., Xu, Y., Zhao, H., Zhang, Z.: Multi-turn dialogue comprehension from a topic-aware perspective (2023). https://arxiv.org/abs/2309.09666
11. Maharana, A., Lee, D.H., Tulyakov, S., Bansal, M., Barbieri, F., Fang, Y.: Evaluating very long-term conversational memory of LLM agents (2024). https://arxiv.org/abs/2402.17753
12. Packer, C., et al.: Memgpt: towards LLMS as operating systems (2024). https://arxiv.org/abs/2310.08560
13. Park, J.S., O'Brien, J.C., Cai, C.J., Morris, M.R., Liang, P., Bernstein, M.S.: Generative agents: interactive simulacra of human behavior (2023). https://arxiv.org/abs/2304.03442
14. Robertson, S., Zaragoza, H., Robertson, S., Zaragoza, H.: the probabilistic relevance framework: bm25 and beyond the probabilistic relevance framework: bm25 and beyond Boston -delft foundations and trends r in information retrieval (2017)
15. Touvron, H., et al.: Llama: open and efficient foundation language models (2023). https://arxiv.org/abs/2302.13971
16. Zhang, C., et al.: A survey on multi-turn interaction capabilities of large language models (2025). https://arxiv.org/abs/2501.09959
17. Zhang, Z., et al.: A survey on the memory mechanism of large language model based agents (2024). https://arxiv.org/abs/2404.13501
18. Zhao, P., et al.: Retrieval-augmented generation for AI-generated content: a survey (2024). https://arxiv.org/abs/2402.19473
19. Zhong, W., Guo, L., Gao, Q., Ye, H., Wang, Y.: Memorybank: enhancing large language models with long-term memory (2023). https://arxiv.org/abs/2305.10250

Author Index

Z. Li et al. (Eds.): CCIR 2025, LNCS 16369, p. 133, 2026.
https://doi.org/10.1007/978-981-95-5637-3

MIX
Papier aus verantwortungsvollen Quellen
Paper from responsible sources
FSC® C105338

If you have any concerns about our products,
you can contact us on
ProductSafety@springernature.com

In case Publisher is established outside the EU,
the EU authorized representative is:
Springer Nature Customer Service Center GmbH
Europaplatz 3, 69115 Heidelberg, Germany

Printed by Libri Plureos GmbH
in Hamburg, Germany